Collector's Encyclopedia of

MADE in JAPAN CERAMICS

FIRST EDITION

Identification
&
Values

Carole Bess White

cb

COLLECTOR BOOKS

A Division of Schroeder Publishing Co., Inc.

Front cover: **Clockwise from left:**
Chef condiment set, page 118, $50.00 – 75.00.
Goldcastle swan candy box, page 214, $35.00 – 45.00.
Lady with suitcase ciggarette set, page 113, $125.00 – 185.00.
Elephant with golf ball cigarette set, page 111, $30.00 – 45.00.
Lady with guitar cigarette set, page 113, $125.00 – 185.00.

Back cover: **Clockwise from left:**
Maruyama lady cigarette set, page 114, $125.00 – 185.00.
Birds and nest salt & pepper set, page 194, $15.00 – 25.00.
Kangaroo & Joey salt & pepper set, page 193, $25.00 – 35.00.
Butler biscuit barrel, page 91, $250.00 – 300.00.
Lady in polka dot pants bowl, page 99, $20.00 – 35.00.
Chicken spice set, page 159, $50.00 – 75.00.

Cover design: Beth Summers
Book design: Kelly Dowdy
Photographer: Leslie M. White

COLLECTOR BOOKS
P.O. Box 3009
Paducah, Kentucky 42002-3009
www.collectorbooks.com

Copyright © 2005 Carole Bess White

The current values in this book should be used only as a guide. They are not
intended to set prices, which vary from one section of the country to another.
Auction prices as well as dealer prices vary greatly and are affected by condition
as well as demand. Neither the author nor the publisher assumes responsibility
for any losses that might be incurred as a result of consulting this guide.

Searching For A Publisher?

We are always looking for people knowledgeable within their fields. If you feel
that there is a real need for a book on your collectible subject and have a large
comprehensive collection, contact Collector Books.

Contents

Acknowledgments 4

About the Author and Photographer 5

1930s Catalog Illustrations 6

The Data

     History of Made in Japan Ceramics 14

     Pricing and the Internet 17

The Backstamps 18

The Collectibles

     Art Deco 45

     Baskets 84

     Bathing Beauties 90

     Biscuit Barrels 91

     Bookends 95

     Bowls 99

     Candleholders 101

     Cigarette and Tobacco Items 104

     Condiment Sets 118

     Cream and Sugar Sets 125

     Figurines 127

     Flower Bowls and Flower Frogs 134

     Incense Burners 140

     Kitchen Items 145

     Liquor Items 161

     Mayonnaise Sets 169

     Muffineer or Berry Sugar and Creamer Sets 171

     Nut Cups or Salt Dips 176

     Pincushions 178

     Planters and Cache Pots 182

     Powder Boxes 190

     Salt and Pepper Sets 191

     Tea & Coffee Items 200

     Toothbrush Holders 203

     Useful Objects 212

     Vases

          Hanging 223

          Standing 225

          Tree 236

     Wall Pockets 240

          Kitchen Wall Pockets 248

Reproductions and Fantasy Items 250

Ceramic Novelties, 1960s – 1990s 251

Bibliography 255

Index 255

Acknowledgments

With this book we are starting a new series that features items never before pictured, as well as old favorites from Volumes 1 through 4 of *The Collectors Guide to Made in Japan Ceramics*, so it seems like a good time to say thank you to all who have shared their wonderful collections for photographing for our books, and for their help, support and advice over the years both in America and Japan

As always, thanks to my husband Dr. Les White, EdD, ace photographer, without whom these books would still be just a gleam in my eye.

Janice Ahl
Joyce Alexander
Larry & Pam Amato
Toshio Ando
Richard Ashley
Lucille Babcock
Betty Bain
Pat & Forrest Bither
Shirley Bolman
Karen Bowers
Ann Brady
Nancy, Bill, Elizabeth & John Brewer
Debbie Wyco Brown —
    dealerofthepast on eBay
Don Buckingham
Colleen Bulger and Ron Torres
Lea & Ron Burcham
Candy Bussell
Sara Butler
Al & Carol Carder
Larry Clark
Debbie and Randy Coe
Dave Coons
Richard Cushing
Billie Dahl
JoAnn & John Dawley
Carrie & Gerry Domitz
Lois Eagan
Kevin Eberhard
Donna Edgar
Jan Edmonston
David Elyea — neatstuffdave on eBay
Susan Farwell
Maureen Fisher — bluelassie on eBay
Dorothy Fiscus
David Flemming
John & Cindy Frank
Jeff Gassner
Joe Gay Dos and Jim Dunk
Jewell Gowan
Eleanor & Peter Groves
Mable Hardebeck

Sheldon & Sayo Harmeling
Fumitaka Hattori
Ron Hankin
Angie Haynes
Arthur Heem, Jr.
Velma & Elmer Heffner
George & Patricia Hill from Lolo, Montana
Lillian Hodges
Dick & Gyrid Hyde-Towle
Linda & Roger Jensen
Aleta Johnson
Carrol & Lucielle Johnson
Sonja Johnston
Yukata Kato
Sara Kelahan
Nirmal Kaur Khalsa
Sewa Singh and Sewa Kaur Khalsa
Michael Kolibaba
Susumo Kondo
Kiyoshi Kosakai
Bonnie Lipsey
Grace & Jim Livingston
Main St. Antique Mall, Los Gatos, California
Karen McGee
Louise Meter
Mike & Sandy Miles
Sandra Millius & Jeff Motsinger
Fern Moist
Pat & Harold Moyer
Bill Naito
Sam Naito
Yashiro Nakano
Tomoko Nakashima
Claudia Navratil
James Neal
Laurel O'Donnell
MaSao Oki
Al & Marguerite Olds
Chris & Chuck Palmer
Floyd Pearson & Skip Schaeffer
Larry & Trudi Peters
Debbie Phillips

Helene Piro
Cathy Pisaneschi
    pennies4later on eBay
Dorothy Polizzi
Bessie & Ernest Proctor
Don & Helen Proctor
Portland's Rain of Glass
Leonard & Margie Reinecke
Janet Richardson
Bernice Robertson
Roger & David
    @ Bettyswollocks*Antiques
Nancy Ronne, PhD
Susan C. Rugh — scrugh on eBay
Agnes Rytkonen
Judy Scott
Seven Gables, Olympia, Washington
Sue & Bob Seymour
Ron Shaffer
Sherrill's Antiques
Neal Skibinski
Deni Smith
Patty & Tim Spencer
Mary Ann and Bob Sloan
David & Jannie Spain

Cheryl Steele
Harvey Steele
Linda & Sam Steward
Keishi Suzuki
Asami Takeuchi
Lucille and Clint Thomas
David J. Trachtenberg—
    victorvictoriana on eBay
Deb Triest
Jim Vanek
W. Joanne Voeller
Bud Walker
Janice Wallace
Jan & Ernie Weaver
Joe Webb
Jim & Kaye Whitaker
Gary White & John Veillette
Dewey & Ann Whited
Betty Whitehall — rosehull on eBay
Aleta Woodruff
Don & Nancy Wright
Laura Enloe Wright
Bonnie Wrozek
Kohei Yoshido

If you have Made in Japan ceramics you would like to see featured in a future book, have information to share or would like autographed copies, please email cbessw@aol.com

About the Author and Photographer

Carole Bess White is the author of six other collector books: *The Collector's Guide to Made in Japan Ceramics*, Volumes 1, 2, 3 and 4, as well as *The Collector's Guide to Lunch Boxes*, and *Glass and Ceramic Baskets*. She has been a serious collector of Made in Japan since 1981. She is also a collector in many other categories including Depression Glass and Elegant Glass, and she is a 1920s and 1930s movie fan. For a number of years she was also a potter, producing wheel-thrown stoneware and raku vessels.

She is a member of the Noritake Society, National Cambridge Collectors, Inc., the Tiffin Glass Collectors Club, and a lifetime member of Portland's Rain of Glass. She is show chair for Rain of Glass and produces two glass-china-pottery shows for them every year.

Research on Made in Japan is a major interest of Carole's, and she will continue her studies in this area.

Les White, EdD, has spent many years working with photography and computers. At present he is the academic coordinator for an area K-12 school.

Les collects nothing but computers!

The Whites reside in Portland, Oregon.

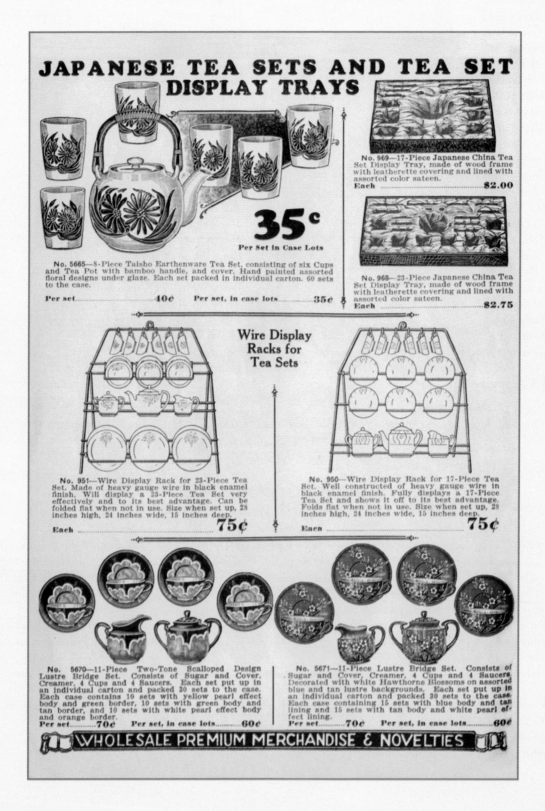

JAPANESE TEA SETS AND TEA SET DISPLAY TRAYS

35¢
Per Set in Case Lots

No. 5665—8-Piece Taisho Earthenware Tea Set, consisting of six Cups and Tea Pot with bamboo handle, and cover. Hand painted assorted floral designs under glaze. Each set packed in individual carton. 60 sets to the case.

Per set............40¢   Per set, in case lots............35¢

No. 969—17-Piece Japanese China Tea Set Display Tray, made of wood frame with leatherette covering and lined with assorted color sateen.
Each $2.00

No. 968—23-Piece Japanese China Tea Set Display Tray, made of wood frame with leatherette covering and lined with assorted color sateen.
Each $2.75

Wire Display Racks for Tea Sets

No. 951—Wire Display Rack for 23-Piece Tea Set. Made of heavy gauge wire in black enamel finish. Will display a 23-Piece Tea Set very effectively and to its best advantage. Can be folded flat when not in use. Size when set up, 28 inches high, 24 inches wide, 15 inches deep.

Each ....**75¢**

No. 950—Wire Display Rack for 17-Piece Tea Set. Well constructed of heavy gauge wire in black enamel finish. Fully displays a 17-Piece Tea Set and shows it off to its best advantage. Folds flat when not in use. Size when set up, 28 inches high, 24 inches wide, 15 inches deep.

Each ....**75¢**

No. 5670—11-Piece Two-Tone Scalloped Design Lustre Bridge Set. Consists of Sugar and Cover, Creamer, 4 Cups and 4 Saucers. Each set put up in an individual carton and packed 30 sets to the case. Each case contains 10 sets with yellow pearl effect body and green border, 10 sets with green body and tan border, and 10 sets with white pearl effect body and orange border.
Per set............70¢   Per set, in case lots............60¢

No. 5671—11-Piece Lustre Bridge Set. Consists of Sugar and Cover, Creamer, 4 Cups and 4 Saucers. Decorated with white Hawthorne Blossoms on assorted blue and tan lustre backgrounds. Each set put up in an individual carton and packed 30 sets to the case. Each case containing 15 sets with blue body and tan lining and 15 sets with tan body and white pearl effect lining.
Per set............70¢   Per set, in case lots............60¢

WHOLESALE PREMIUM MERCHANDISE & NOVELTIES

Imported Earthenware Tea and Beverage Sets

STAR VALUES
LOWEST PRICES

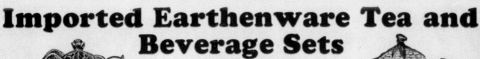

No. 5685 — Imported Japanese Beverage or Lemonade Set. Consisting of a hard-baked earthenware, lustre finish pitcher, beautifully decorated and painted in contrasting colors, with six cups to match. Height of pitcher, 9 inches; height of cup, 3½ inches. Each set in individual carton. Packed 36 sets to the case.

Each	75¢
Each, in case lots	65¢

No. 5684 — Imported Japanese Beverage or Lemonade Set. Consists of a hard-baked earthenware pitcher and six cups with handles, attractively decorated and painted in yellow and green colors, that resembles an ear of corn. Height of pitcher, 6½ inches; height of cup, 3 inches. Each set in an individual carton. Packed 36 sets to the case.

Each	75¢
Each, in case lots	65¢

55¢
Per Set in Case Lots

55¢
Per Set in Case Lots

11-Piece Taisho Tea Set

No. 5678 — 11-Piece Taisho Earthenware Tea Set. Consists of six Cups, Tea Pot with cover and bamboo handle, Sugar with cover and Creamer. Hand painted floral designs under glaze. Each set put up in individual carton. Packed 60 sets to the case. An exceptionally good selling tea set and fine value at our low price.

Per set	60¢
Per set, in case lots	55¢

No. 5677 — Barrel Design 8-Piece Taisho Earthenware Set. Highly glazed finish Tea Pot with six Cups to match and black colored hoops. Packed each in an individual carton and 60 sets to the case. Each case contains 40 Green colored sets and 20 Brown colored sets.

Per set	50¢
Per set, in case lots	45¢

No. 5676 — 8-Piece Taisho Earthenware Tea Set, consisting of Tea Pot with bamboo handle and six Cups to match. Decorated with hand painted floral design on cream colored, glazed basket weave finish body with black striped trimming. Packed each set in an individual carton and 60 sets to the case.

Per set	45¢
Per set, in case lots	40¢

WHOLESALE PREMIUM MERCHANDISE & NOVELTIES

IMPORTED EARTHENWARE LEMONADE SETS AND REFRIGERATOR SETS

Orangeade Set

Lemonade Set

No. 5686—Japanese Earthenware 8-Piece Orangeade Set. Consists of pitcher with handle and orange reamer which serves as cover and strainer, and six cups to match. Highly glazed finish with assorted color raised floral decorations on attractive pebbled surface body. Packed each set in an individual carton, and 60 sets to the case.

Per set...60¢
Per set, in case lots................................55¢

No. 5687—Imported 8-Piece Earthenware Lemonade Set. Highly glazed finish tall shape pitcher with handle and lemon reamer which serves as cover and strainer, and six cups to match. Beautifully hand painted with assorted color floral decorations on cream color body. Packed each set in an individual carton, and 60 sets to the case.

Per set...60¢
Per set, in case lots................................55¢

No. 5766—Japanese Nested Refrigerator Set. Glazed finish and decorated with hand painted floral design in assorted colors. Each set consists of three containers made of hard baked earthenware, each with a fitted cover. Size of individual containers, 6 inches in diameter and 4⅛ inches high; 4⅜ inches in diameter and 3⅜ inches high; 3⅝ inches in diameter and 3 inches high. Packed 2 sets in a carton, and 6 doz. sets to the case.

Per dozen sets...............$5.75
Per doz. sets, in case lots...$5.50

No. 5767—Imported Japanese Refrigerator Set. Consisting of three containers, each with a fitted cover, made of hard baked earthenware. Attractively decorated with hand painted floral designs in assorted colors. Size of individual containers, 5 inches in diameter and 3½ inches high; 4¼ inches in diameter and 2½ inches high; 3½ inches in diameter and 2 inches high. Packed 2 sets in a carton, and 8 dozen sets to the case.

Per dozen sets..............$4.25
Dozen sets, in case lots....$4.00

No. 5765—Imported Japanese Nested Refrigerator Set. Beautifully decorated with hand painted floral designs in assorted colors. Each set consists of three containers made of hard baked earthenware, each with a fitted cover and knob handle. Size of individual containers, 6 inches in diameter and 4⅜ inches high; 5 inches in diameter and 3⅜ inches high; 4 inches in diameter and 2⅞ inches high. Packed 2 sets to the carton, and 6 dozen sets to the shipping case.

Per dozen sets...............$5.75
Per doz. sets, in case lots...$5.50

WHOLESALE PREMIUM MERCHANDISE & NOVELTIES

Japanese Earthenware Refrigerator Sets

Attractively Decorated

No. 5764—Imported Japanese Square Shaped Nested Refrigerator Set. Consisting of three containers, each with a fitted cover and knob handle, made of hard baked earthenware with assorted color hand painted floral designs on white body. Size of individual containers, 5 inches square and 4¾ inches high; 4 inches square and 3¾ inches high; 3¾ inches square and 2½ inches high. Packed 2 sets in a carton and 5 dozen sets to the case.

Per dozen sets..................$6.25
Per dozen sets, in case
    lots $6.00

No. 5760—Imported Japanese Nested Refrigerator Set. Three containers made of hard baked earthenware each with a fitted cover and grooved handle, to the set. Hand painted raised cherry design in assorted colors on basket weave finish cream colored body. Size of individual containers, 6 inches in diameter and 4¾ inches high; 4¾ inches in diameter and 3½ inches high; 3¾ inches in diameter and 3 inches high. Packed 2 sets in a carton and 6 dozen sets to the case.

Per dozen sets..................$6.00
Per dozen sets, in case lots....$5.75

No. 5761—Japanese Triangular Shaped Nested Refrigerator Set. Each set consists of three hard baked earthenware containers each with a fitted cover and knob handle. Attractively decorated with hand painted floral designs in assorted colors on white body. Size of individual containers, 7 inches in diameter and 4¾ inches high; 5¾ inches in diameter and 3¾ inches high; 4¼ inches in diameter and 2¾ inches high. Packed 2 sets in a carton and 5 dozen sets to the case.

Per dozen sets..................$6.10
Per dozen sets, in case
    lots $5.85

No. 5762—Japanese Octagon Shaped Refrigerator Set. Decorated with hand painted raised floral design in assorted colors on basket weave finish, two-tone colored body. Each set consists of three containers made of hard baked earthenware in octagon shape. Size of individual containers, 5¼ inches in diameter and 4¾ inches high; 4¾ inches in diameter and 3¾ inches high; 3½ inches in diameter and 2½ inches high. Packed 2 patterns assorted in a carton and 6 dozen sets to the case.

Per dozen sets..................$6.00
Per dozen sets, in case
    lots $5.75

No. 5759—Extra Large Size Imported Japanese Cookie Jar. Made of hard baked earthenware with assorted colored hand painted raised floral designs on cream colored glazed body. Complete with detachable bamboo handle and fitted cover. 8 inches in diameter and 8½ inches high (not including handle). Packed each in an individual carton and 3 dozen to the case.

Per dozen $7.75
Per dozen, in case lots..........$7.50

No. 5763—Imported Japanese Nested Refrigerator Set. Glazed finish, hand painted, assorted colored floral designs on green and yellow octagon shaped body. Three containers made of hard baked earthenware, each with a fitted cover, to the set. Size of individual containers, 5¼ inches in diameter and 4¾ inches high; 4¾ inches in diameter and 3½ inches high; 3½ inches in diameter and 2½ inches high. Packed 2 sets in a carton and 6 dozen sets to the case.

Per dozen sets..................$6.10
Per dozen sets, in case
    lots $5.85

WHOLESALE PREMIUM MERCHANDISE & NOVELTIES

IMPORTED JAPANESE COOKIE JARS
A CHOICE SELECTION AT
LOWEST PRICES

No. 5753—Barrel Design Japanese Cookie Jar. Made of hard baked earthenware in green and brown, highly glazed finish with black colored hoops. Complete with cover and detachable bamboo handle. Height, 6½ inches (not including handle). Packed each in an individual carton and 5 dozen to the case. Each case contains 3½ dozen green and 1½ dozen brown cookie jars.

Per dozen.................................$5.15
Per dozen, in case lots........$4.90

No. 5755—Japanese Imported Cookie Jar. Made of hard baked earthenware, attractively decorated with hand painted assorted color raised floral design on cream color glazed basket weave finish body. Complete with detachable bamboo handle and cover. Height, 7 inches (not including handle). Packed each in an individual carton and 5 dozen to the case.

Per dozen $5.75
Per dozen, in case lots..... $5.50

No. 5756 — Clown Design Imported China Cookie Jar. Three-tone glazed finish body, highly decorated and hand painted with gilt knobs. Complete with cover and detachable bamboo handle. Height, 7 inches (not including handle). Packed each in an individual carton and 6⅔ dozen to the case.

Per dozen $6.00
Per dozen, in case lots........$5.75

No. 5754—Imported Japanese Cookie Jar. Lustre finish body in assorted colors with scalloped design, made of hard baked earthenware. Attractively decorated with assorted color, hand painted raised flower designs. Octagon shape with detachable bamboo handle and cover. Height, 8 inches (not including handle). Packed each in an individual carton and 5 dozen to the case.

Per dozen $5.75
Per dozen, in case lots........$5.50

No. 5757—Octagon Shape Imported Cookie Jar. Made of hard baked earthenware with hand painted raised flower designs in assorted colors on highly glazed basket weave finish body. Complete with detachable bamboo handle and cover. Height, 7¼ inches (not including handle). Packed each in an individual carton and 5 dozen to the case. Each case contains 3½ dozen green and 1½ dozen yellow lustre finish cookie jars.

Per dozen.................................$6.25
Per dozen, in case lots.................$6.00

No. 5752 — Imported Japanese Cookie Jar. Made of hard baked earthenware with hand painted moulded and raised assorted color flower designs on glazed cream color body with striped trimmings. Complete with cover, fancy knobs, and bamboo handle. Height, 7 inches (not including handle). Packed each in an individual carton and 5 dozen to the case.

Per dozen.................................$4.75
Per dozen, in case lots........$4.50

No. 5750—Japanese Imported Cookie Jar. Made of hard baked earthenware, octagon shape, cleverly designed in satsuma decorations with contrasting backgrounds of black and brown colors. Hand painted with gilt knobs and trimmings. Complete with detachable bamboo handle and cover. Height, 6½ inches (not including handle). Each in individual carton. Packed 60 to the case.

Per dozen.................................$8.00

No. 5751—Japanese Imported Cookie Jar. Made of hard baked earthenware in octagon shape, green color body with gilt knobs and border. Beautiful raised surface of Japanese scene in rich colors. Complete with detachable bamboo handle and cover. Height, 6½ inches (not including handle). Each in individual carton. Packed 60 to the case.

Per dozen $8.00

WHOLESALE PREMIUM MERCHANDISE & NOVELTIES

JAPANESE CHINA TEA POTS, COOKIE
Jars, Cups and Saucers

No. 5673 — Japanese China Cup and Saucer. New style Two-Tone Lustre Scalloped design. Put up in sets of 6 cups and 6 saucers to the carton. Size of cup 3¾x2 inches, saucer 5½ inches. Packed 60 sets to case, each case containing an equal assortment of three color combinations.

Per set .... 50¢
Per set, in case lots .... 45¢

No. 5672 — Japanese China Cup and Saucer. Made in assorted blue and tan lustre colors. Put up in sets of 6 cups and 6 saucers to the carton. Size of cup 3¾x2 inches, saucer 5½ inches. Packed 60 assorted color sets to case.

Per set .... 45¢
Per set, in case lots .... 40¢

No. 5674 — Japanese China Cup and Saucer. Assorted Blue and Tan Lustre colors, decorated with white Hawthorne Blossoms. Put up in sets of 6 cups and 6 saucers to the carton. Size of cup 3¾x2 inches, saucer 5½ inches. Packed 60 assorted color sets to case.

Per set .... 50¢
Per set, in case lots .... 45¢

No. 5679 — Japanese Earthenware Tea Pot. Made of hard baked earthenware highly glazed in octagon shape. Beautifully decorated with hand painted raised floral designs in assorted colors. Length, 9 inches; height, 6 inches. Packed two in a carton (no less sold) and 6 dozen to the case. Each case contains a complete assortment of colors.
Per dozen $3.50

No. 5675 — Imported Japanese Earthenware Tea Pot. Highly glazed basket weave finish body, attractively decorated with hand painted raised fruit and floral design and brown striped trimming. Length, 8¾ inches; height, 6¾ inches. Packed two in a carton (no less sold) and 6 dozen to the case.
Per dozen $3.50

No. 5681 — Japanese Novelty Elephant Tea Pot. Made of hard-baked earthenware with white body and beautifully painted blanket in bright colors, gilt-painted features with black and red figure of boy sitting on cover. Complete with bamboo handle and cover. Length, 8 inches; height, 7 inches (not including handle). Put up two in box. (No less sold.) Packed 84 in case.
Per dozen $3.50

No. 5758 — Large Size Japanese Cookie Jar. Made of hard-baked earthenware, attractively decorated with assorted colored hand painted floral decorations on two-tone and three-tone glazed body with gilt knobs. Complete with detachable bamboo handle and cover. Height, 8 inches (not including handle). Packed each in an individual carton and 4 dozen to the case. Each case contains three assorted designs.
Per dozen $7.00
Per dozen, in case lots $6.75

No. 5682 — Japanese Novelty Elephant Tea Pot. Made of hard-baked earthenware with white body and nicely painted features. Cleverly designed elephant with trunk turned upward. Complete with detachable bamboo handle and cover. Length, 8 inches; height, 6¼ inches (not including handle). Put up two in box. (No less sold.) Packed 96 in case.
Per dozen $3.75

No. 5680 — Japanese Novelty Elephant Tea Pot. Made of hard-baked earthenware in elephant shape with satsuma decorations. Has gilt trimmings with bright red and assorted color features and attractive decorations on brown background. An extremely rich coloring effect all over tea pot. Length, 9¾ inches; height, 7¼ inches. Put up two in box. (No less sold.) Packed 72 in case.
Per dozen $5.25

No. 5683 — Japanese Novelty Camel Tea Pot. Made of hard-baked earthenware in camel shape with delicate green and yellow color background, and bright color decorations. Complete with stained wicker handle and cover. Length, 9¼ inches; height, 6¼ inches (not including handle). Put up two in box. (No less sold.) Packed 72 in case.
Per dozen $5.75

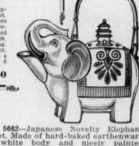

WHOLESALE PREMIUM MERCHANDISE & NOVELTIES

JAPANESE CHINA NOVELTY ASH TRAYS

Medium Size Dice Ash Tray
No. 5181—Imported Japanese Dice Ash Tray. An exact imitation of a large round cornered dice with large top opening and four grooved cigar rests. Highly glazed white china with Black colored spots. Size, 2½x2½ in. Packed one dozen in box.
Per dozen............................35¢
Per gross.........................$3.75

Small Size Dice Ash Tray
No. 5180—Japanese China Dice Ash Tray. Exactly the same as the large Dice Ash Tray but smaller in size. Supplied with assorted colored spots in Black, Green, Red and Blue painted on white glazed body. Size, 2x2 inches. Packed one dozen assorted colors in box.
Per dozen............................25¢
Per gross.........................$2.75

Large Size Dice Ash Tray
No. 5155—Imported Japanese Dice Ash Tray, made of highly glazed white porcelain, with spots in assorted Black, Green, Red and Blue colors, to resemble a large round cornered dice. Has large top opening with four grooved cigar rests. Diameter, 2¾x2¾ inches. Packed one dozen assorted colors in box.
Per dozen............................50¢
Per gross.........................$5.50

No. 3107—Novelty Condiment or Ash Tray Set. Made of glazed white Japanese China with wooden lid on center bowl and two small size pots with handles attached at either side, with inscriptions as illustrated. Height, 2½ inches; width, 3¾ inches.
Per dozen............................70¢
Per gross.........................$8.00

No. 5182—Imported Bridge Ash Tray. Made of Japanese China in high lustre finish and consists of three round cornered, square shaped trays attached. Center tray has four grooved cigarette rests. Painted with designs representing card suits on all sides, and inscriptions on front as illustrated. Length, 5½ inches; height, 2½ inches. One dozen in box.
Per dozen............................65¢
Per gross.........................$7.50

No. 5102 — Novelty Japanese Lustre China Ash Trays. Assorted Bathing Girl and Clown figures, with brightly colored features, boat shape design. Length, 5½ inches. Packed one dozen assorted styles in box.
Per dozen............................65¢
Per gross.........................$7.20

No. 5115—Japanese China Elephant Ash Tray. Satsuma decorated and hand painted with gilt trimmings on brown-colored background. Has lavishly gilt decorated match and cigarette holders on each side. Length, 7 inches; height, 4½ inches. Packed one in a box.
Per dozen.........................$5.75

Novelty Out-House Ash Tray
No. 3127—Imported China Out-House Ash Tray. Consists of a brightly painted oval shaped tray with an orange colored out-house and two colored boys at one end. A new and very amusing novelty. Height, 2½ inches. Packed one dozen in box.
Per dozen............................65¢
Per gross.........................$7.20

No. 5128 — Novelty Japanese Lustre China Ash Tray. Highly glazed figure of Bulldog, tinted in bright and attractive colors. Length, 4½ inches; height, 3 inches. Packed one dozen in box.
Per dozen............................85¢

WHOLESALE PREMIUM MERCHANDISE & NOVELTIES

NOVEL JAPANESE CIGARETTE HOLDERS AND ASH TRAYS

No. 5144—Japanese China Ash Trays and Cigarette Holder Assortment. Lustre finish triangular shaped tray in assorted colors with brightly painted animals seated at end. Average width, 4½ inches. Packed one dozen assorted subjects and colors to the box.

Per dozen ....65¢
Per gross $7.20

No. 5132—Novelty Japanese China Ash Tray and Cigarette Holder. Made of highly glazed china with animal figure of a Rino in standing position over ash tray. Bright colored spots on the cream body create an attractive color combination. Height, 2¾ inches. Packed one dozen in box.

Per dozen .... **75¢**

No. 5130 — Novelty Japanese China Ash Tray and Cigarette Holder. Made of highly glazed china with animal figure of a sheep in bright color combination on soft color body. Height, 3 inches. Packed one dozen in box.

Per dozen ....65¢
Per gross $7.20

No. 5122 — Novelty Japanese Imported Ash Tray. Made of highly glazed china with Hawaiian figure in sitting position, tinted in bright and attractive colored features with blue color leaf shape ash tray. Height, 3½ inches. Packed one dozen in box.

Per dozen ....65¢
Per gross $7.50

No. 5101—Novelty Japanese Lustre China Ash Tray and Cigarette Holders. Made in assorted bright color combinations, with comical animal white china figures, with tinted color features. Average length, 4 inches. Packed one dozen assorted styles to box.

Per dozen ....65¢
Per gross $7.20

No. 5123—Imported Japanese Novelty Ash Tray. Made of highly glazed china with figure of standing cat tinted in attractive colored features with green lustre base. Height, 3½ inches; width, 4 inches. One dozen in box.

Per dozen ....70¢
Per gross $8.00

No. 5140—Imported China Ash Trays and Cigarette Holders. Supplied in assorted shapes and colors with attractively painted figure of bathing girl in various poses seated at end. Average length, 3 inches. Packed one dozen assorted colors and designs to the box.

Per dozen ....40¢
Per gross $4.75

No. 5131—Novelty Japanese China Ash Tray and Cigarette Holder. Made of highly glazed china in lustrous finish with bright color combinations with figure of horse in sitting position exactly as illustrated. Height, 3⅜ inches. Packed one dozen in box.

Per dozen ....65¢
Per gross $7.20

No. 5104—Japanese China Ash Tray and Cigarette Holder Assortment. Highly glazed trays in assorted colors and shapes with brightly painted figures of dogs and cats seated at end. Average length, 3 inches. Packed one dozen assorted colors and subjects to the box.

Per dozen ....45¢
Per gross $4.75

WHOLESALE PREMIUM MERCHANDISE & NOVELTIES

The Data
History of Made in Japan Ceramics

By American law, imported pieces are required to be marked with their country of origin. The changes in this law that Congress enacted over the years help the collectors of today determine when their pieces were made:

1860s – 1891	**JAPONISME ERA** All types of Japanese art and ceramics were eagerly collected in the West. Before 1891, goods exported to America did not have to be stamped with their country of origin in English. Japanese ceramics usually had no backstamps, or they had artists' or their patrons' names in Japanese characters.
1891 – 1921	**NIPPON/HAND PAINTED NIPPON ERA** The McKinley Tariff, which took effect March 1, 1891, required that all imported goods had to be stamped in English with their country of origin. At the time, "Nippon" was considered to be an acceptable name for Japan, so most Japanese ceramics of this period were backstamped "Nippon" or "Hand Painted Nippon," often with a company logo as well. However, not all were stamped that way. There were still unmarked pieces, and pieces stamped "Japan" as well. Nippon pieces are priced higher than Made in Japan and are eagerly sought by collectors.
1921 – 1941	**NORITAKE ART DECO ERA** Many collectors consider the Noritake Art Deco pieces the "Cadillac" of Made in Japan ceramics. They were consistently of better quality and most beautifully decorated, and today they are very avidly collected and are priced accordingly! Noritake Art Deco pieces generally are priced higher than similar Made in Japan pieces.
1921 – 941	**EARLY MADE IN JAPAN ERA ("GOLDEN AGE")** The U.S. Customs Bureau ruled that "Nippon" was no longer an acceptable synonym. As of August 1, 1921, all goods were supposed to be backstamped "Japan" or "Made in Japan." Technically, the MIJ Era began when the Nippon era ended in 1921, but it really was not that precise. At some point the U.S. Customs Bureau may have required that the words "Made In" be added to the backstamps, but this was not always done. Unmarked pieces sometimes slipped through Customs, but most of the ceramics from 1921 to 1941 are marked either "Japan" or "Made in Japan." Sometimes, all pieces in a set are not backstamped. The profit margin on ceramics was slim, and a factory could save a little labor cost by not marking every piece in a set. If pieces in a set have different backstamps, it is because there often was not room for "Made in Japan," or a company logo, so they just used "Japan" on some of the smaller pieces. Early Made in Japan pieces, especially Art Deco and lustres, have come into their own and are very collectible.
	THERE WAS AN EMBARGO ON JAPANESE IMPORTS DURING WORLD WAR II, SO NO NEW SHIPMENTS OF JAPANESE CERAMICS WERE IMPORTED FROM 1941 UNTIL THE END OF THE WAR. PIECES ALREADY IN AMERICA CONTINUED TO SELL. IT TOOK NEARLY TWO YEARS FOR THE FIRST JAPANESE CERAMICS TO REACH AMERICA AFTER THE WAR ENDED.
1947 – 1952	**OCCUPIED JAPAN/MADE IN OCCUPIED JAPAN ERA** The United States occupied Japan from September 2, 1945, until April 28, 1952. The Occupied Japan backstamp Era truly began August 15, 1947, when the first shipment of Occupied Japan arrived in America. The U.S. Customs Bureau decreed in 1949 that Japanese goods could be marked "Occupied Japan," "Made in Occupied Japan," "Japan, " or "Made in Japan." Again, some were not marked at all. Occupied ware has its ardent collectors as well, but prices seem to be about equal to or (in some cases) lower than early Made in Japan.
1952 – TODAY	**POST-WAR MADE IN JAPAN ERA** When the Occupation ended in 1952, marks no longer contained the word "Occupied," so pieces were again marked only with "Japan" or "Made in Japan." This is when the paper label era really began. Prior to WW II, paper labels were flimsy and the glue was often not strong, so the Customs Bureau usually made importers replace the labels with indelible ink backstamps. In the 1950s, technology improved and paper labels were allowed. The two most common types of labels seem to be: ✻ Small oval or rectangular blue or black paper with white letters ✻ Two-color metallic, such as black or red with gold or silver lettering The real sleepers are the post-WW II Made in Japan pieces because they are still very affordable!

Ceramics were produced in Japan long before the periods of interest to this book, which are 1921 to 1941, and 1952 to the present:

Japonisme Era (1860s – 1891)

Prior to the 1860s, Japan was a closed country and traded with the West only through the Dutch. Commodore Perry was sent by the United States government to open trade relations with Japan. The ceramics exported from the 1860s to the 1890s bear little resemblance to the ceramic dishes and novelties in this book. (Japanese manufacturers refer to almost everything that is not a dish as a novelty.) The pieces were artistic, rustic, folk — Imari, Kutani, Arita, etc. — but they were not the little "dogs on ashtrays" types of pieces that we know, love and collect today.

The Japanese exhibit at the Exposition Universelle in Paris in 1867 introduced Japanese objets d'art to an amazed and fascinated public. A Japanese style craze swept the Western world. Art, architecture, music, literature, and, of course, ceramics were all avidly studied and collected. The French named this movement Japonisme, and its influence lasted late into the nineteenth century.

By the time the United States marking law had changed in 1891 to require the country of origin in English, the supply of Japanese ceramics had begun to grow to meet the demand, but it was still more of a cottage industry than not. Pieces from this period were still made in the Japanese style; in other words, the teacups had no handles.

Nippon Era (1891 – 1921)

The Nippon Era began when the U.S. mandated that imports had to be marked with their country of origin. In Japan, Noritake and a few smaller companies began production of more commercial types of Western-style dishes and novelties; in other words, the teacups now had handles. Originally, Japanese novelties were copies of German originals, but as techniques improved and experience grew, a far wider variety was produced.

German "original" Christian Fischer Wall Pocket, 9¼" tall, $500.00.

Early Made in Japan Era (1921 – 1941)

By the 1920s, Japan was exporting ceramics to many countries, but German and eventually Czech ceramics were in the forefront in America. When World War I broke out and the United States could no longer trade with Germany, Japan was poised and ready to step up their production of ceramic dishes and novelties. America's Great Depression of the 1930s with its terrible economic conditions opened the door for inexpensive imported dishes and novelties from Japan.

German "original" Bellhop Cigarette Holder, marked "4657 Germany," 4" tall, $35.00 – 55.00.

German "original" Bunny Basket, marked "6454A Germany," 3¼" tall, $25.00 – 35.00.

The "golden age" of Made in Japan ceramics was 1929 to 1939. During this time, the popularity of ceramic dishes and novelties "from the Orient" reached its peak. They were affordable and colorful, and the largest numbers of what many collectors today consider to be the most creative, interesting and desirable collectibles were made during this time. It was the age of luster glazing, long before it was known that the ingredients used to make it were harmful. The Art Deco ceramics produced by the Noritake Company during the 1920s and 1930s are considered by many collectors to be premium pieces, with higher prices. But other companies produced interesting and varied designs as well in Art Deco and other styles.

By 1939, the U.S. economy had improved and styles were changing. Although Americans still continued to buy Japanese dishes and novelties, the designs were no longer as Art Deco-influenced or as charmingly naïve as the earlier pieces, and luster was losing popularity.

And then came World War II. With the bombing of Pearl Harbor on December 7, 1941, Japan became the enemy of America and all Japanese imports were embargoed, including ceramics. Many Americans expressed their patriotism by refusing to buy the remaining pre-embargo Japanese items, or by buying them to smash.

Czech "original" Wall Pocket, marked "MT Czechoslovakia," $30.00 – 45.00.

Occupied Japan Era

After the War ended, America occupied Japan from 1945 until 1952. Only industries that would help rebuild the economy yet which could not possibly help Japan to re-arm were permitted, and the ceramics industry was perfect for this. Production resumed, and the first large shipment of Occupied Japan ceramics arrived in New York on August 15, 1947.

New pieces were designed, but older pre-WWII styles were re-created as well. Most of the molds had been melted down for war material, but any that survived may have been re-used. This makes it challenging for collectors to date pieces.

1952 – Present

The ceramics industry enjoyed many profitable years after World War II. Styles at first resembled the older, pre-War ware, but as time went on, they changed to reflect their decades. Gradually things changed in Japan as better-paying jobs in the electronics and automotive industries became available. Today, very few ceramic novelties are imported to America from Japan; most of the ceramic output for the American market is china, such as Noritake and Mikasa.

Pricing and the Internet

For collectors and sellers alike, the Internet is fun and profitable. And it's not going away. There are pluses and minuses. The big benefit is that it's open all hours, all days. The Internet brings the things we love into our homes in a way that we never could have envisioned a few years ago. Items from all over the world are right there on our computer screens.

There can be bargains galore on Internet sites, and most transactions are highly satisfactory. But not all — pieces arrive with damage that the seller overlooked or chose not to disclose, or packed so badly that they broke in transit, or were just plain stomped by the post office. And sometimes we just pay more than we want to either because of auction fever, or because, even with the greater number of pieces available to us on the Internet, they're still not making that stuff anymore.

The question is: should the Internet auction price determine the value of an item? Not really, because it's too much like a worldwide rummage sale. There are bargains to be had, but when this happens it's just the same as getting lucky at a garage sale down the street.

Say you find a piece at a tag sale for a dollar. But you have seen it in books, and at shows and shops, priced in the neighborhood of $50.00. Do you value it at $1.00 for insurance? Obviously not! How much are you going to ask for it if you are buying it for resale? Are you going to double your money and offer it for $2.00? Again, obviously not! What you are going to do is dance like Rumplestiltskin for the joy of the bargain, then price it accordingly!

When an Internet auction ends, the price on the screen may or may not be the final one, depending on whether or not there is a reserve. If there is a reserve on the piece and it is not met, the final cost may be privately negotiated between the buyer and seller, and other interested parties don't have access to their decision and therefore have no idea what value was put on it. And sometimes things do not sell within the allotted time period of their auction, usually five to ten days and then it's over unless the seller relists the item. Does this mean that item is no longer desirable? No, it is just like putting merchandise in a shop. Maybe the right buyer will come along within five to ten days after you put it out, or maybe not. In a shop, you just sit and wait. On the Internet, you relist immediately or later, but the principle is the same. But the fact that the item did not sell really has no effect on the value — it's just luck of the draw.

Time after time the same item will go really high, then sharply drop off because the few people who really wanted it and were willing to pay big bucks for it finally all have it, leaving the next seller scratching his head and wondering why his piece did not sell as high as the previous ones.

And don't forget — the final amount you pay on the Internet has to include shipping and insurance, as well as the selling price of the piece. For example:

Wall Pocket on the Internet	$19.89
Postage	8.00
Insurance	1.30
Total	$29.19

It's tempting to think of that pocket as costing only $19.89, but in reality you are paying almost $30.00 for it!

So where does the answer lie? Book prices have to take into consideration all venues: the Internet, shops, shows, and flea markets, as well as replacement costs for insurance purposes. On the one hand, Internet prices even with postage can be lower than shop and show prices, depending on how many folks are willing to bid on the item — kind of like a tag or garage sale. In that case it might look like Internet prices are about ½ to ¼ of book prices. But on the other hand, things can go really high — all it takes is two crazy bidders both wanting the same item. Really, it's between the buyer and the seller — what the piece is worth to you.

Rarity

In earlier books, some items were designated as "rare." If the Internet has done nothing else, at least it has made even the scarcest items accessible, so we will no longer refer to them as "rare."

The Backstamps

There were *thousands* of different marks used on Made in Japan ceramics over the years. Japanese manufacturers, exporters, importers and American retail sellers could mark pieces however they preferred, as long as they contained the words "Japan" or "Made in Japan."

Because of the huge number of marks and labels, we show only those on pieces in this book, and in Volumes 1 through 4 of *The Collectors Guide to Made in Japan Ceramics*. If your piece has a different mark than one shown here, that does not necessarily make it rare just because it's not "in the book." It usually just means that it was not used on a piece that we have featured in one of our books. Plus, not all of the marks shown will be found on pieces in every one of our books as we list them cumulatively.

MARKS 1--4, 40 No specific company — nearly all companies used variations of these marks at one time or another	**MARK 58, 58a** Nagoya Boeki Shokai, still in business
	MARK 59 Nanri Boeki & Co., closed 1978
MARKS 5-9, 13-19, 22, 23A, 27, 29, 33-39, 41, 46, 50, 52, 55, 56, 62, 62A, 66, 67, 72-74, 76-98, 100-103, 105-110, 112-140 unknown	**MARKS 60, 60a, 61** Mogi Shoji & Co., still in business
MARK 10 Shofu Industrial Co., Ltd., in business before WWII, closed September of 1965	**MARK 63** Yokoi Sei-Ichi Shoten closed 1942
MARKS 11, 12, 21, 21a, 21b, 32,43, 43a, 44 Tashiro Shoten Ltd., in business before WWII, closed 1954	**MARK 64, 75** Nagoya Seito Sho (mark 64) started business c. 1908, was purchased by Sumimoto Steel Industry Company c. WWII, and the name was changed to Narumi Seito Sho (Mark 75 was registered in 1934). Narumi is still in business.
MARKS 20, 24, 25, 30, 30A Seiei & Co., in business before WWII, closed 1962 (Mark 30A was registered in 1932.)	
MARK 23 Nihon Yoko Boeki Co., still in business	**MARK 65** Yamashiro Ryuhei (later changed to Maruyama Toki), opened in 1914, stopped production 1989
MARKS 26, 36, 53, 53a, 54 Nippon Toki Kasha (Noritake Co., limited) founded 1876 still in business	**MARK 68** Iwata (could be name of manufacturer or exporter), closing date unknown
MARK 28 Hotta Yu Shoten & Co., in business before WWII, closed 1947	
	MARKS 69 & 70 Manufactured in Japan for the American Company, Joséf Original, from 1955 through the early 1970s
MARK 31 Maruka Tajimi Boeki Shokai, still in business	
MARK 42 Enesco, Japan, closed November 1978	**MARK 71** Aichi Toki Shokai (formerly Higo Hoten), still in business
MARK 45 Hanai Giryo Co., in business before WWII, closing date unknown	**MARK 81** ESD is Lefton's Canadian mark
MARKS 47 & 48 Tsujiso Toki Co. In Book 1, mark #44 was substituted for mark #48. mark #48 is correct in this book and Book 2.	**MARK 99** Shimizu-rokunosuko Shoten, Nagoya, registered this mark in 1932. They closed before WWII.
MARK 49 Kinkozan, 1645 – 1927	**MARK 104** Marugo Seito Sho Inc., Tokoname City, Aichi Prefecture, registered this mark in 1950. They stopped production in the 1980s.
MARK 57 United China & Gift Co. (formerly United China & Glass Co.), still in business	
"Toki" is Japanese for Chinaware or pottery, and "Kaisha" is company	**MARKS 111, 111A** Empire Trading Co., Ltd., Nagoya, which had no factory, registered this mark in 1950. They closed their business in the 1980s.

Mark 1

Mark 2

Mark 3

Mark 4

Mark 5

Mark 6

Mark 7

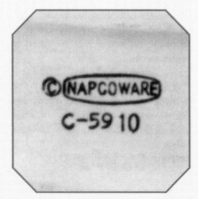

Mark 8

Mark 9

Mark 10

Mark 11

Mark 12

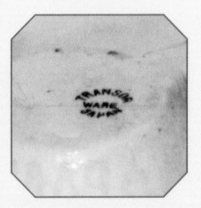

Mark 13

Mark 14

Mark 15

Mark 16

Mark 17

Mark 18

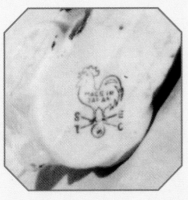

Mark 19

Mark 20

Mark 21

Mark 21A

Mark 21B

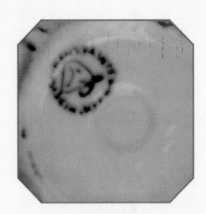

Mark 21C

Mark 22

Mark 23

Mark 23A

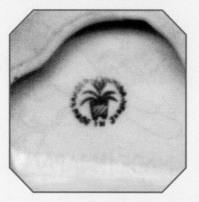

Mark 23B

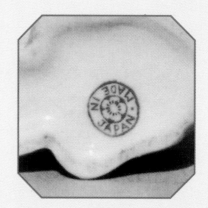

Mark 24

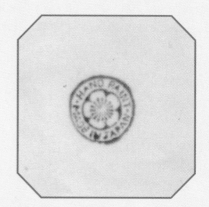

Mark 25

Mark 26

Mark 27

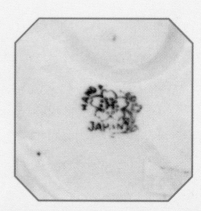

Mark 28. Top line says hand painted

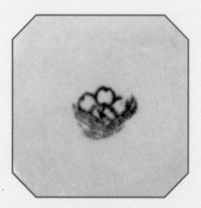

Mark 29

Mark 30

Mark 30A

Mark 30B

Mark 31

Mark 32

Mark 32A

Mark 33

Mark 34

Mark 35

Mark 35A

Mark 36

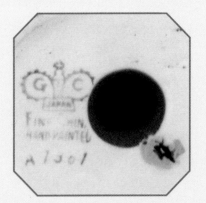

Mark 37

Mark 38

Mark 38A

Mark 39

Mark 40

Mark 41

Mark 42

Mark 43

Mark 43A

Mark 44

Mark 45

Mark 46

Mark 47

Mark 48

Mark 49

Mark 50

Mark 51

Mark 51A

Mark 52

Mark 53

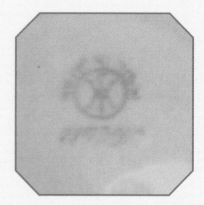

Mark 53A

Mark 53B

Mark 54

Mark 55

Mark 56

Mark 57

Mark 57A

Mark 57B

Mark 57C

Mark 57D

Mark 58

Mark 58A

Mark 59

Mark 60

Mark 60A

Mark 61

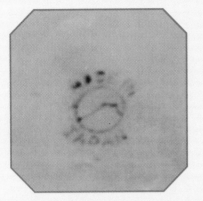

Mark 62

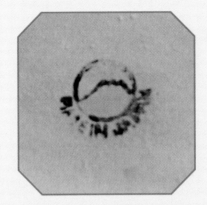

Mark 62A

Mark 63

Mark 64

Mark 64A

Mark 65

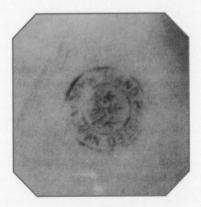

Mark 66

Mark 66A

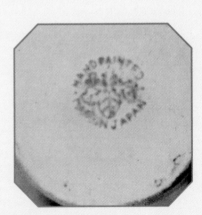

Mark 66B

Mark 66C

Mark 66D

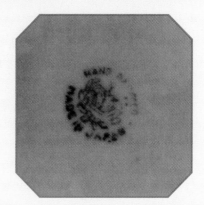

Mark 67

Mark 68

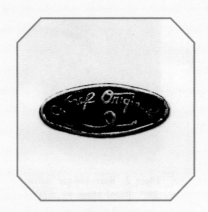

Mark 69

Mark 70

Mark 71

Mark 72

Mark 73

Mark 73A

Mark 74

Mark 75

Mark 76

Mark 77

Mark 78

Mark 79

Mark 79A

Mark 80

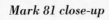
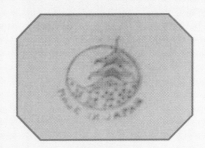

Mark 81 *Mark 81 close-up* *Mark 82*

Mark 83 *Mark 84* *Mark 85*

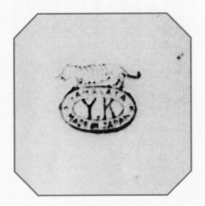

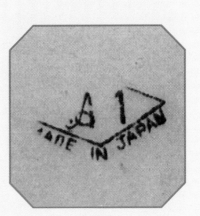

Mark 86 *Mark 87* *Mark 88*

Mark 89

Mark 90

Mark 91

Mark 91A

MADE IN JAPAN

KP

KIEJIRI

CO

YOKKAICHI

Mark 92

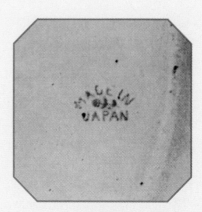

Mark 93

Mark 94

Mark 95

Mark 95A

Mark 96

Mark 97

Mark 98

Mark 99

Mark 100

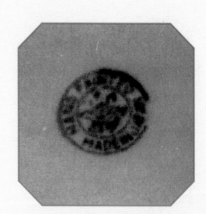

Mark 101

Mark 102

Mark 103

Mark 104

Mark 105

Mark 106

Mark 107

Mark 108

Mark 108A

Mark 109

Mark 110

Mark 111

Mark 111A

Mark 112

Mark 112A

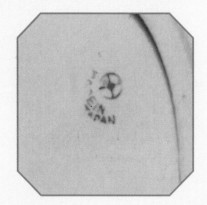

Mark 113

Mark 114

Mark 115

Mark 116

Mark 117

Mark 118

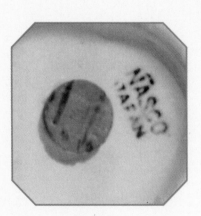

Mark 119

Mark 120

Mark 121

Mark 122

Mark 123

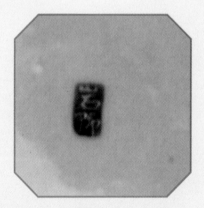

Mark 124

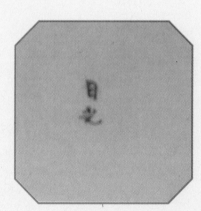

Mark 125

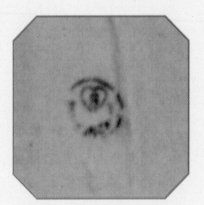

Mark 126

Mark 126A

Mark 127

Mark 128

Mark 129

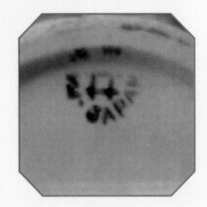

Mark 130

Mark 131

Mark 132

Mark 133

Mark 134

Mark 134A

Mark 135

Mark 136

Mark 137

Mark 138

Mark 138A

Mark 139

Mark 140

Mark 141

Mark 142

Mark 143

Mark 144

Mark 145

Mark 146

Mark 147

Mark 148

Mark 149

Mark 150

Mark 151

Mark 152

Mark 153

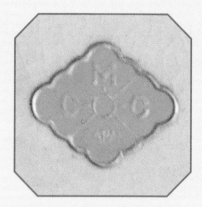

Mark 154

Mark 155

Mark 156

Mark 157

Mark 158

Mark 159

Mark 160

Mark 161

Mark 162

Mark 163

Mark 164

Mark 165

Mark 166

Mark 167

Mark 168

Mark 169

Mark 170

Mark 171

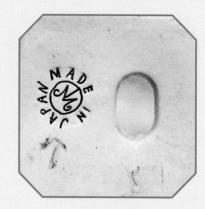

Mark 172

Mark 173

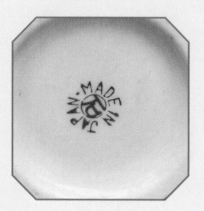

Mark 174

Mark 175

Mark 176

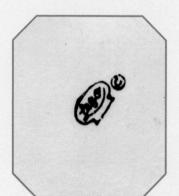

Mark 177

Mark 178

Mark 179

Mark 180

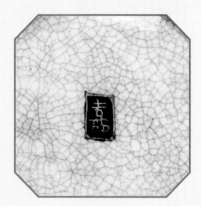

Mark 181

Mark 182

Mark 183

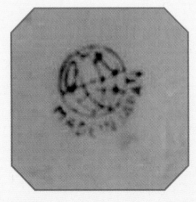

Mark 184

Mark 185

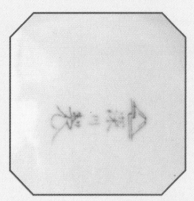

Mark 186

Mark 187

Mark 188

Mark 189

The Collectibles

Measurements are rounded off to the nearest quarter-inch. Even though the ink color of the backstamps is not an indication of age, it is included anyway where possible.

The naming of pieces' functions is based on catalogs, research, direct knowledge, or comparison with similar objects. However, what the actual function was meant to be is often lost to us today, and in truth, many items were sold in wholesale catalogs in assortments and didn't always have names on each piece. Also, items were sold with multiple functions, depending on what was popular with consumers at the time, or with no function at all — just another geegaw for the knickknack shelf. So my pincushion might be a toothpick holder to you and a plant rooter to your grandmother. Last we heard there were no "function police" to arrest us for misnaming, so if it's your piece, you can call it whatever you like.

Some items are noted as Akiyama, or Akiyama-style, pieces. The Akiyama family had Oriental gift stores in Portland, Oregon, from the 1920s until 1942. They were interned for the duration of World War II, so they stored the remaining stock in the basement of their house. It stayed there until 1987, when Hanji Akiyama, their son, sold the house and placed the pieces in a local antique mall.

Other items are noted as found in Butler Brothers wholesale catalogs of the 1920s and 1930s. Butler Brothers catalogs are wonderful period references for everything — not just Made in Japan. Still others are noted as found in the Sears catalog, which is, of course Sears Roebuck. The Sears catalogs can be found on microfilm in several public libraries — ask your librarian for help.

The main types of glazes used on Made in Japan ceramics are luster (metallic or pearly overglaze); shiny (glossy); matte (flat, opaque with no shine); semi-matte (opaque with some shine); and cold paint, which is subject to flaking. Bisque pieces usually have cold paint on them, but sometimes they have fired-on glazes.

This book, along with Volumes 1 – 4 of *The Collector's Guide to Made in Japan Ceramics*, gives an overview of as many types as possible of the thousands of Made in Japan ceramic collectibles made over the years.

Art Deco

Plate 1. *Set of four dog ashtrays with match or place card holders, in multicolored luster glazes with silhouette scenic motif, 3¾" tall, all black mark #1, $90.00 – 130.00 set.*

Plate 2. *Ashtray with downhill skier in multicolored shiny glazes, 4½" wide, red mark #1, $60.00 – 85.00.*

Plate 3. *Niagara Falls souvenir ashtray with black cat in multicolored luster and shiny glazes, 3" tall, green mark #1, $20.00 – 35.00.*

Plate 4. *Basket in multicolored luster and shiny glazes with striped motif in oil spot glaze, 7" tall, red mark #20, $50.00 – 75.00.*

Plate 5. *Basket with red flower in multicolored luster and shiny glazes, 3½" tall, red mark #20, $20.00 – 25.00.*

Plate 6. *Goldcastle basket with gazelle-like handle in multicolored luster and shiny glazes, 7¾" long, red mark #43, $20.00 – 35.00.*

Plate 7. *Card suit biscuit barrel in multicolored shiny glazes, 5½" tall, red mark #25, $50.00 – 80.00.*

Plate 8. *Biscuit barrel with German-style air-brushed geometric motif in multicolored shiny glazes, black mark #88, 6" tall, $50.00 – 80.00.*

Plate 9. *Bookends with Mexican motif in multicolored shiny glazes, 5" tall, red mark #2, $45.00 – 65.00.*

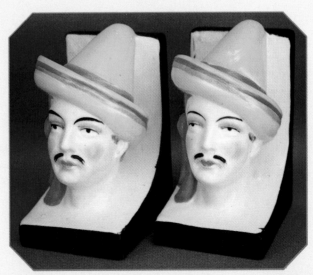

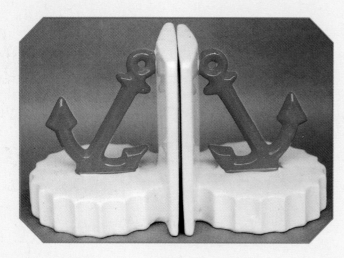

Plate 10. *Anchor bookends in cream and orange shiny glazes, 4¾" tall, red mark #24, $35.00 – 45.00.*

Plate 11. *Trico flower or bulb bowl in multicolored luster glazes with floral motif, 7½" wide, red mark #12, $20.00 – 35.00.*

Plate 12. *Flower or bulb bowl with fish in multicolored luster glazes, 7½" wide, red mark #25, $95.00 – 100.00.*

Plate 13. *Large salad or serving bowl in multicolored luster glazes, 9½" wide, green mark #52, $35.00 – 55.00.*

Plate 14. *Bowl with cat handle in multicolored luster glazes, 7" wide, red mark #1, $30.00 – 55.00.*

Plate 15. *Bowl with geometric motif in multicolored luster glazes, reed handle, 8" wide, red mark #25, $25.00 – 45.00.*

Plate 16. *Box with Asian motif in multicolored shiny glazes, $65.00 – 75.00.*

Plate 17. *Maruyama Scottie cache pot in cream and red shiny glazes, 4½" tall, red mark #65, $25.00 – 35.00.*

Plate 18. *Cache pot with umbrella girl in blue and white shiny glazes, 5¾" tall, black mark #2, $20.00 – 35.00.*

Plate 19. *Green cat cache pot in multicolored shiny glazes, 3¾" tall, blind mark #1, $20.00 – 35.00.*

Plate 20. *Cat open candy dish in multicolored luster glazes, shown in a 1920s Butler Bros. Wholesale Catalog for 65¢ wholesale – $1.00 $1.50 retail, 4¼" tall, black mark #1, $50.00 – 75.00.*

Plate 21. *Elephant covered candy box in white and multicolored shiny glazes, 8¾" tall, red mark #67, $75.00 – 125.00.*

Plate 22. *Cat covered candy box in blue and tan luster glazes, 6¾" tall, red mark #1, $90.00 – 110.00.*

Plate 23. *Covered candy box supported by a pair of dogs in a rare design of multicolored luster glazes, a pre-WWII piece from the Akiyama store, 7¾" tall, black mark #1, $175.00 – 255.00.*

Plate 24. *Urn-style covered candy jar in multicolored luster and shiny glazes, pictured in the Fall 1930 Sears Roebuck catalog with a similar decoration for $1.00, 7½" tall, red mark #25, $60.00 – 80.00.*

Plate 25. *Covered sectional candy box in multicolored shiny glazes, 4¼" tall, red mark #1, $60.00 – 80.00.*

Plate 26. *Clown covered cigarette box in multicolored luster and shiny glazes, 5½" tall, black mark #1, as pictured, $95.00 – 125.00 (with four stacking ashtrays, $125.00 – 175.00).*

Plate 27. *Cigarette box and ashtray set with fish in multicolored shiny glazes, 3¾" tall, red mark #66c, $55.00 – 75.00.*

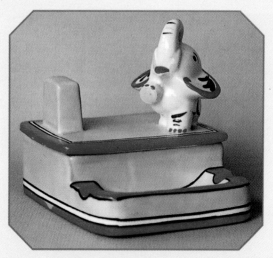

Plate 28. *Cigarette box with calico elephant and attached ashtray in multicolored shiny glazes, 4½" tall, black mark #1, $45.00 – 60.00 as pictured ($75.00 – 85.00 with set of four stacking ashtrays).*

Plate 29. *Calico elephant cigarette box with matchbox holder in multicolored luster glazes, 5½" tall, black mark #1, $65.00 – 100.00.*

Plate 30. *Cigarette box with mystery animal knob in multicolored crackle glazes, 5" tall, red mark #1 with "CB10SS," $55.00 – 80.00.*

Plate 31. *Cigarette box with cat in multicolored luster glazes (see matching ashtray in catalog on page 13 of this book), 3¾" wide, black mark #1, $50.00 – 70.00.*

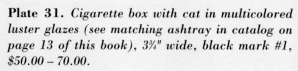

Plate 32. *(Left) Clown cigarette box with attached match holder in multicolored luster glazes, 5" tall, black mark #1, $50.00 – 55.00 as pictured ($70.00 – 85.00 with four stacking ashtrays under his collar); (right) Asian man match or cigarette box with attached ashtray, 6" tall, red mark #25, $65.00 – 95.00.*

Plate 33. *Winking man cigarette holder in multicolored luster and shiny glazes, 5" tall. red mark #1, $40.00 – 60.00.*

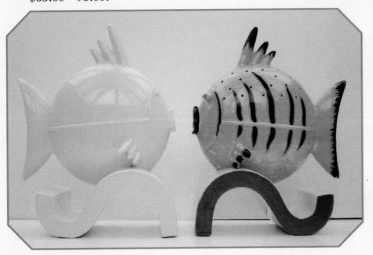

Plate 34. *Two fish cocktail pick holders in multicolored shiny glazes, 8" tall, (left) red mark #2, $25.00 – 45.00; (right) red mark #66c, $55.00 – 65.00.*

Plate 35. *Maruyama maid with eggs condiment set in multicolored luster glazes, 5" tall, red mark # #65, $85.00 – 125.00 (purchased in Australia).*

Plate 36. *Black cat and castle condiment set in multicolored shiny glazes pictured in the Fall-Winter 1931 Sears Roebuck catalog for $1.00, red mark #25 on base, red mark #1 on pieces, $125.00 – 150.00. (The Noritake Company made a better-quality version of this piece.)*

Plate 37. *Condiment set and drippings jar in multicolored shiny glazes, cruets 6½" tall, all red mark #66c, set, $75.00 – 85.00 as pictured ($85.00 – 100.00 with undertray for condiment set).*

Plate 38. *Cream and sugar set with rabbit handles and scenic motif in multicolored luster and shiny glazes, 3¾" tall, black mark #1, $30.00 – 45.00 set.*

Plate 39. *Trico batwing lady figurine in butterscotch and multicolored shiny glazes, 7" tall, mark #11, $85.00 – 125.00.*

Plate 40. *Batwing lady figurine in pink and multicolored shiny glazes, 7½" tall, red mark #1, $85.00 – 125.00.*

Plate 41. *Batwing lady figurine in green and multicolored shiny glazes, 10½" tall, unmarked, $125.00 – 150.00.*

Size comparison of batwing ladies.

Plate 42. *Tall Moriyama bathing suit lady with hat and dog figurine in multicolored shiny glazes, 12½" tall, red mark #65, $125.00 – 150.00.*

Plate 43. *Spanish lady with fruit basket figurine in multicolored shiny glazes, 6½" tall, red mark #57, $35.00 – 50.00.*

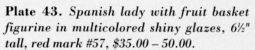

Plate 44. *Goldscheider-style girl and boy figurine in multicolored shiny glazes, 8½" tall, red mark #2, $45.00 – 65.00.*

Plate 45. *Goldscheider-style skier figurine in multicolored shiny glazes, 6½" tall, red mark #2, $45.00 – 65.00.*

Plate 46. *Large Goldscheider-style bust by Kent Art Ware in white shiny glaze, 10" tall, black mark #166, $85.00 – 125.00.*

Plate 47. *Kent Art Ware lady on horse figurine in white shiny glaze, 9½" tall, black mark #166, $85.00 – 125.00.*

Plate 48. *Pair of ram's head figurines in white shiny glaze, both blue mark #1; (left) 9" tall, $35.00 – 55.00; (right) 7½" tall, $30.00 – 50.00.*

Plate 49. *Log dinosaur in green and white shiny glazes, 2½" tall, red mark #2, $18.00 – 28.00.*

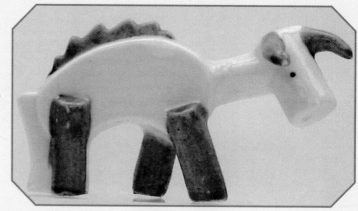

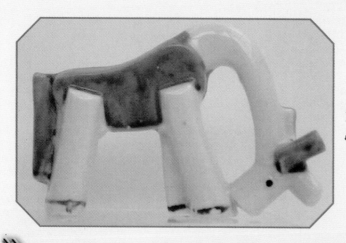

Plate 50. *Log giraffe in green and white shiny glazes, 2½" tall, red mark #2, $18.00 – 28.00.*

Plate 51. *Humidor in multicolored crackle glazes, 6" tall, red mark #25, $45.00 – 65.00 (As opposed to a tobacco or cigarette jar, a humidor has a compartment in the lid for a dampened sponge to keep the tobacco moist).*

Plate 52. *Marmalade or jam jar with matching plate and spoon in multicolored luster and shiny glazes, jar and spoon, red mark #1; plate, red mark #66D; $30.00 – 45.00.*

Plate 53. *Mayonnaise set in multicolored shiny glazes, 3¾" tall, black mark #1, $40.00 – 75.00.*

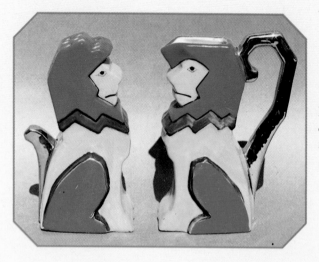

Plate 54. *Lion muffineer or berry sugar and creamer set in multicolored luster and shiny glazes, red mark #67, $95.00 – 135.00.*

Plate 55. *Muffineer or berry sugar and creamer set in multicolored luster and shiny glazes, 5¾" tall, red mark #20, $45.00 – 55.00.*

Plate 56. *Square muffineer or berry sugar and creamer set in multicolored luster and shiny glazes, 5½" tall, red mark #24, $45.00 – 55.00.*

Plate 57. *Muffineer or berry sugar and creamer set with pagoda motif in multicolored shiny glazes, 6" tall, black mark #1 in an oval, $45.00 – 55.00.*

Plate 58. *Muffineer or berry sugar and creamer set with screw top in teal and multicolored luster glazes, 6½" tall, red mark #52, $45.00 – 55.00.*

Plate 59. *Cat napkin ring in multicolored luster glazes, 2¾" tall, no mark, $25.00 – 35.00.*

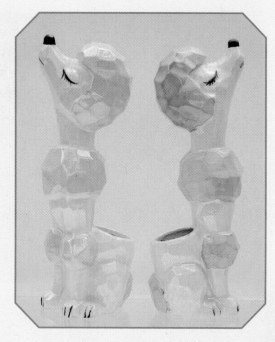

Plate 60. *A pair of French poodles with attitude, pincushions in multicolored luster glazes, black mark #2, $30.00 – 40.00 each.*

Plate 61. *A trio of Trico pitchers with geometric motifs in multicolored shiny glazes, 4½" tall, mark #12, $25.00 – 40.00 each.*

Plate 62. *Two pitchers: (left) Covered syrup with matching underplate in multicolored luster and shiny glazes, 6¼" tall, plate, blue mark #1 and red mark #25; pitcher, red mark #25, $55.00 – 75.00; (right) Jug in multicolored semi-matte glazes, 6" tall, red mark #26, $40.00 – 55.00 with this or other Art Deco motif (with a non-Deco motif, reduce the price to $15.00 – 20.00).*

Plate 63. *Place card holder in multicolored shiny glazes, 3" tall, red mark #1 and blind mark #1, $38.00 – 48.00.*

Plate 64. *Pair of Scottie dog plaques in multicolored shiny glazes, 4" tall, red mark #1, $50.00 – 75.00 set.*

Plate 65. *Pair of planters or cache pots with shamrock motif in multicolored shiny glazes, (left) 4" tall, $20.00 – 30.00; (right) 4¾" tall, $30.00 – 40.00; both black mark #72.*

Plate 66. *Powder jar in cream and multicolored luster glazes, 4½" diameter, red mark #12, $45.00 – 65.00.*

Plate 67. *Clown powder jar in multicolored luster glazes, 7¼" tall, red mark #1, $175.00 – 275.00.*

Plate 68. *Pair of powder jars in multicolored luster glazes, (left) skirt holder, 5½" tall, black mark #1, $75.00 – 125.00; (right) clown, 5¼" tall, black mark #1, $100.00 – 125.00.*

Plate 69. *Googly-eyed children in bathing suits with inner tubes, salt and pepper set in multicolored shiny glazes, 3" tall, red mark #1, $42.00 – 52.00.*

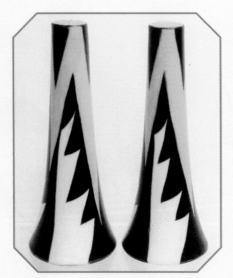

Plate 70. *Tall salt and pepper set with geometric motif in multicolored shiny glazes, 4" tall, green mark #1, $20.00 – 35.00.*

Plate 71. *Salt and pepper set with geometric motif in blue and white luster glazes, $20.00 – 35.00.*

Plate 72. *Salt and pepper set in the form of whistling teakettles in black and white shiny glazes with "HOLLYWOOD CALIF." decal, 2¾" tall, black mark #2, $20.00 – 35.00.*

Plate 73. *Salt and pepper set with muffineer or berry sugar and creamer set in black and white luster glazes; (left and right) 6½" tall, red mark #1, $65.00 – 85.00 set; (center) 5¼" tall, black mark #1, $20.00 – 35.00 set.*

Plate 74. *Spoon holder in multicolored luster glazes, 4¾" long, black mark #1, $35.00 – 45.00.*

Plate 75. *Tea set in black and white luster glazes, all red mark #1; teapot, 8" tall, $65.00 – 95.00; cream and sugar set, 6" tall, $35.00 – 45.00.*

Plate 76. *Tea set in multicolored luster glazes; teapot, 7", red mark #24, $65.00 – 95.00; small muffineer or berry sugar and creamer set, 3½" tall, $45.00 – 65.00.*

Plate 77. *Tea set on tray in multicolored luster and shiny glazes with oilspot panels and enameling, pot 5" tall, all red mark #25, set, $75.00 – 100.00.*

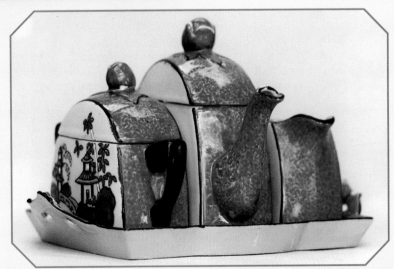

Plate 78. *Tea set in red and white shiny glazes; (from left) teapot on tile, 6" tall, red mark #12a, $65.00 – 95.00 set; cream and sugar set on tray, 6¾" wide, red mark #23a, $45.00 – 55.00 set.*

Plate 79. *Teapot on tile in multicolored luster glazes with triangle motif, pot, 7¾" tall, all red mark #25, $45.00 – 65.00 set.*

Plate 80. *Tea and hot water set on tray in multicolored luster glazes, 4¼" tall, all black mark #1, $45.00 – 75.00 set.*

Plate 81. *Tea and hot water set on tray in multicolored luster glazes, tray, 6" wide, red mark #28, $45.00 – 75.00 set.*

Plate 82. *Oval tray in multicolored luster glazes, 10½" wide, black mark #1, $25.00 – 45.00.*

Plate 83. *Trico vase with geometric and floral motif in multicolored luster glazes, 7½" tall, red mark #12, $75.00 – 125.00.*

Plate 84. *Vase with floral motif in multicolored luster glazes, 7½" tall, $75.00 – 125.00.*

Plate 85. *Goldcastle vase with sweeping handles in multicolored matte glazes, 8" tall, red mark #43, $75.00 – 125.00.*

Plate 86. *Goldcastle vase in red, white, blue, and multicolored luster and shiny glazes, 8½" tall, red mark #43, $75.00 – 125.00.*

Plate 87. *Trico vase with sweeping handles in multicolored luster and shiny glazes, 7½" tall, red mark #12a, $75.00 – 125.00.*

Plate 88. *Trico vase with three pillars in multicolored luster glazes, 7½" tall, red mark #12a, $75.00 – 125.00.*

Plate 89. *Vase with three pillars in multicolored luster glazes, 7¼" tall, black mark #1, $75.00 – 125.00.*

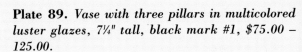

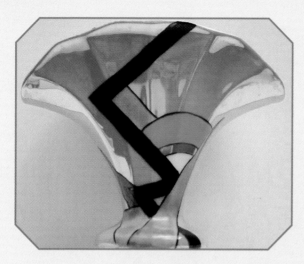

Plate 90. *Fan vase with geometric motif in multi-colored luster glazes, $75.00 – 125.00.*

Plate 91. *Fan vase with floral motif in multicol-ored luster and shiny glazes, 7" tall, green mark #31, $65.00 – 85.00.*

Plate 92. *Fan vase with floral motif in multicolored luster and matte glazes, 6½" tall, red mark #21, $65.00 – 85.00.*

Plate 93. *Vase with floral motif in multicolored luster and matte glazes, 6" tall, green mark #21a, $50.00 – 60.00.*

Plate 94. *Vase with scenic motif in multicolored luster glazes, 7½" tall, no mark, $75.00 – 125.00.*

Plate 95. *Vase with scenic motif in the style of Clarice Cliff in multicolored luster glazes, 7" tall, red mark #20, $75.00 – 125.00.*

Plate 96. *Vase with drip motif in multicolored luster glazes, 8½" tall, black mark #1, $75.00 – 125.00.*

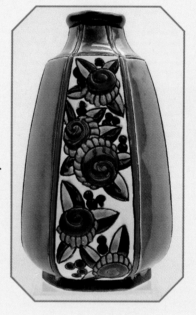

Plate 97. *Vase with floral motif in the style of Charles Catteau, 7½" tall, black mark #35a, $75.00 – 125.00.*

Plate 98. *Square vase with floral motif in multicolored luster glazes, 5" tall, black mark #21c, $75.00 – 125.00.*

Plate 99. *Vase with floral motif in blue and multicolored luster glazes, 6¾" tall, red mark #11, $75.00 – 125.00.*

Plate 100. *Goldcastle vase with lotus motif in multicolored luster glazes, a pre-WWII piece from the owner's family, 6¼" tall, red mark #43, $55.00 – 75.00.*

Plate 101. *Vase with red berries on handles in multicolored luster and shiny glazes, 6¼" tall, red mark #25, $35.00 – 55.00.*

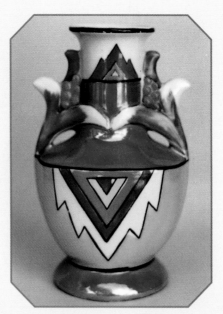

Plate 102. *Ladies and gentlemen vases in multi-colored luster and shiny glazes, 5¼" tall, both black mark #1, $30.00 – 45.00 each.*

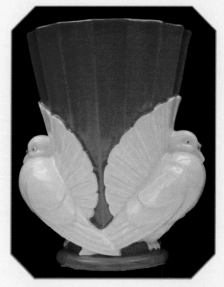

Plate 103. *Vase with doves in multicolored luster and shiny glazes, black mark #50.00, $45.00 – 65.00.*

Plate 104. *Vase with handles and floral motif in multicolored shiny glazes, a pre-WWII piece from the Akiyama store, 5½" tall, black mark #1, blind mark #1, $125.00 – 135.00.*

Plate 105. *(Left) Geometric vase in multicolored shiny glazes, shown in the 1929 Sears Roebuck catalog for 59¢, 7¼" tall, black mark #1, $25.00 – 40.00; (right) handled stacked rings vase in blue and white semi-matte glazes, 5¾" tall, black mark #1, $20.00 – 35.00.*

Plate 106. *Kinkozan vase with autumn leaf motif in black and orange semi-matte glazes, 7½" tall, red mark #49, $85.00 – 135.00.*

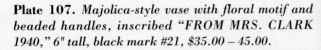

Plate 107. *Majolica-style vase with floral motif and beaded handles, inscribed "FROM MRS. CLARK 1940," 6" tall, black mark #21, $35.00 – 45.00.*

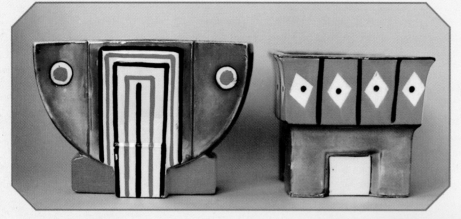

Plate 108. *Two vases in orange and blue shiny glazes: (left) 4¾" tall, red mark #25; (right) 5½" tall, red mark #25, $50.00 – 65.00 each.*

Plate 109. *Two fan vases in green and white semi-matte glazes: (left) 8" tall, (right) 6½" tall, $50.00 – 75.00 each.*

Plate 110. *Hanging vase with flower frog top in multicolored luster glazes with oilspot panels, 5¾" tall, red mark #1, $75.00 – 125.00.*

Plate 111. *Lady head wall hangings in multicolored shiny glazes, 4½" tall, black mark #1, $30.00 – 40.00 each.*

Plate 112. *Goldcastle high style lady head wall hangings in multicolored shiny glazes, 6¾" tall, black mark #43 and blind mark #65, $50.00 – 75.00 each.*

Plate 113. *Lady head wall hanging in multicolored shiny glazes, $75.00 – 100.00.*

Plate 114. *Bacchus wall pocket in aqua shiny glaze, 7" tall, black mark #1, $55.00 – 85.00.*

Plate 115. *Deco Revival wall pocket by Clay Art of San Francisco, 11" wide, silver Clay Art label damaged beyond reading, $25.00 – 35.00.*

Plate 116. *Blue wall pocket with floral motif, 9½" tall, black mark #1, $55.00 – 85.00.*

Plate 117. *Wall pocket with pink rose motif in multi-colored luster glazes, 8½" tall, red mark #20, $35.00 – 45.00.*

Plate 118. *Wall pocket with floral motif in multicol-ored shiny glazes, 6½" tall, blind mark #1, $45.00 – 55.00.*

Plate 119. *Kinkozan tumble-up water set in red and multicolored shiny glazes, jug, 6¼", red mark #49; tumble-up, 4" tall, red mark #49; $55.00 – 80.00 set.*

Plate 120. *Double basket with lady in lavender dress, 5" tall, red mark #2, $15.00 – 25.00.*

Plate 121. *Large basket with sprigged-on bird and flowers in multicolored shiny glazes, 11" tall, blind mark #1, $35.00 – 55.00.*

Plate 122. *Basket with bird in multicolored shiny glazes, 5½" tall, no mark, $30.00 – 40.00.*

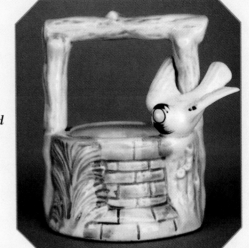

Plate 123. *Bird on well basket in multicolored shiny glazes, 5" tall, red mark #2, $15.00 – $25.00.*

Plate 124. *Bird on watering can basket in multicolored shiny glazes, 3" tall, black mark #2, $15.00 – $25.00.*

Plate 125. *Rooster & Roses basket in multicolored shiny glazes, 5" tall, green mark #57a, $25.00 – 45.00.*

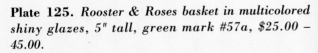

Plate 126. *Small basket in yellow and multicolored shiny glazes, 3½" tall, blind mark #1, $15.00 – 20.00.*

Plate 127. *Norcrest basket with blue flowers, 3½" tall, mark #138a without "Made in Japan" but with numbers "8/337," $15.00 – 20.00.*

Plate 128. *White basket with red roses in multicolored shiny glazes, 4¼" tall, gold mark #2, $15.00 – 20.00.*

Plate 129. *Mid-century moderne basket in multi-colored shiny glazes, 5" tall, green mark #57, $15.00 – 20.00.*

Plate 130. *Flower-shaped basket in multicolored shiny glazes, 2½" tall, black mark #167, $15.00 – 25.00.*

Plate 131. *Tall white basket with pink roses, 5" tall, no mark, $10.00 – 15.00.*

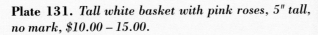

Plate 132. *Pink bucket basket, 4" tall, red mark #2, $10.00 – 15.00.*

Plate 133. *Noritake basket with pagoda motif in multicolored shiny glazes, 3¼" tall, red mark #53, $30.00 – 45.00.*

Plate 134. *Noritake basket in multicolored luster glazes, red mark #54, $35.00 – 50.00.*

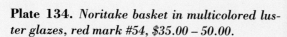

Plate 135. *Maruhon Ware majolica-style basket with lily of the valley motif in multicolored shiny glazes, 6¼" tall, mark #35, $25.00 – 35.00.*

Plate 136. *Round majolica-style basket with floral motif in multicolored shiny glazes, 7" tall, black mark #35, $65.00 – 85.00.*

Plate 137. *Majolica-style basket with fruits in multicolored shiny glazes, 6¾" tall, black mark #1, $65.00 – 85.00.*

Plate 138. *Three mini baskets in multicolored shiny glazes: (left) 2", no mark; (center) 2½", red mark #2; (right) 2", black mark #1; $5.00 – $8.00 each.*

Plate 139. *Three mini baskets in multicolored shiny glazes: (left) 2½" black mark #2; (center) 2", black mark #2; (right) 2", red mark #2; $5.00 – 8.00 each.*

Plate 140. *Maruyama beauty on shell in multicolored luster and shiny glazes, 2¾" tall, red mark #65, $45.00 – 65.00.*

Plate 141. *Beauty on turtle in multicolored shiny glazes, 4¼" tall, black mark #1, $45.00 – 65.00.*

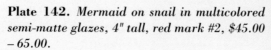

Plate 142. *Mermaid on snail in multicolored semi-matte glazes, 4" tall, red mark #2, $45.00 – 65.00.*

Plate 143. *Bisque mermaid in multicolored semi-matte glazes, 4¾" wide, black mark #2, $45.00 – 65.00.*

Plate 144. *Butler biscuit barrel in multicolored shiny glazes, 9½" tall, mark #2, $250.00 – 300.00.*

Plate 145. *Biscuit barrel with maroon and orange poppies, 8" tall, mark #29, $30.00 – 55.00.*

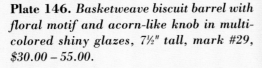

Plate 146. *Basketweave biscuit barrel with floral motif and acorn-like knob in multi-colored shiny glazes, 7½" tall, mark #29, $30.00 – 55.00.*

Plate 147. *Biscuit barrel in white and yellow shiny glazes, 4¼" tall, green mark #1, $20.00 – 45.00.*

Plate 148. *Biscuit barrel similar to Noritake "White & Gold" pattern and from the same period, 7¾" tall, red mark #50, $30.00 – 55.00.*

Plate 149. *(Left) Majolica-style biscuit barrel in multicolored shiny glazes with raised floral motif, 7" tall, black mark #1; (right) majolica-style biscuit barrel in multicolored shiny glazes with basketweave and floral motif, 8" tall; $30.00 – 55.00 each.*

Plate 150. *(Left) Majolica-style bis-cuit barrel with raised floral motif in multicolored shiny glazes, similar to Coors Rosebud ware, 8" tall, black mark #1; (right) majolica-style biscuit barrel in multicolored shiny glazes with fruit motif, 6½" tall, blind mark #1; $30.00 – 55.00 each.*

Plate 151. *(Left) Large majolica-style biscuit barrel in green and multicolored shiny glazes, 8" tall, $30.00 – 55.00; (right) small majolica-style biscuit barrel in multi-colored shiny glazes with stippled texture, 4½" tall, $20.00 – 45.00.*

Plate 152. *(Left) Majolica-style biscuit barrel in yellow and multi-colored shiny glazes, 6¾" tall, black mark #1; (right) majolica-style bis-cuit barrel in multicolored shiny glazes with fruit motif, 5¾" tall, black mark #24; $30.00 – 55.00 each.*

Plate 153. *(Left) Biscuit barrel in orange and multicolored shiny glazes, 6¼" tall, red mark #11, $30.00 – 55.00; (right) large biscuit barrel in green and multicolored shiny glazes with fruit motif, 8" tall, blind mark #88, $30.00 – 55.00.*

Plate 154. *(Left) Imitation Belleek biscuit barrel with green shamrocks on cream basketweave base, 5¼" tall, black mark #1; (right) majolica-style biscuit barrel with green cherry blossom motif, similar to Moriyama ware but raised, 5½" tall, black mark #29; $30.00 – 55.00 each.*

Plate 155. *Mini biscuit barrel in multicolored luster glazes, black mark #133, $20.00 – 35.00.*

Bookends

Plate 156. *"Hans & Greta" bookends in multicolored, cold-painted glazes, 6¼" tall, black mark #78, but the "JAPAN" label is missing, $28.00 – 38.00 pair.*

Plate 157. *Asian couple bookends in multi-colored shiny glazes, 5½" tall, green mark #1, $28.00 – 38.00 pair.*

Plate 158. *Girl and boy bookends in multicolored shiny glazes, 5½" tall, black mark #2, $28.00 – 38.00 pair.*

Plate 159. *Siesta figural bookends in multicolored luster and shiny glazes, 4¼" tall, black mark #2, $28.00 – 48.00 pair.*

Plate 160. *Siesta with cactus bookends in brown and multicolored shiny glazes over brown clay body, 6¼" tall, label #134a, $20.00 – 35.00 pair.*

Plate 161. *Bird bookends in multicolored shiny glazes, 5" tall, label #108, $20.00 – 30.00 pair.*

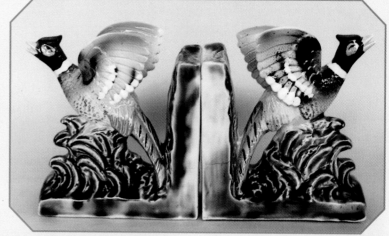

Plate 162. *Dog and doghouse bookends in multicolored shiny glazes, 4¼" tall, black mark #1, $28.00 – 48.00 pair.*

Plate 163. *Dog and doghouse bookends in multicolored shiny glazes, 5¾" tall, label #108a, $28.00 – 48.00 pair.*

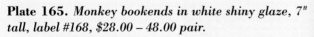

Plate 164. *Dog bookends in green airbrush-style glaze, 5" tall, black mark #2, $28.00 – 48.00.*

Plate 165. *Monkey bookends in white shiny glaze, 7" tall, label #168, $28.00 – 48.00 pair.*

Plate 166. *Horse bookends in green shiny glaze, 7¼" tall, label #169, $15.00 – 25.00 pair.*

Plate 167. *Large elephant bookends in multicolored shiny glazes, 7¼" tall, black mark #1, $28.00 – 48.00 pair.*

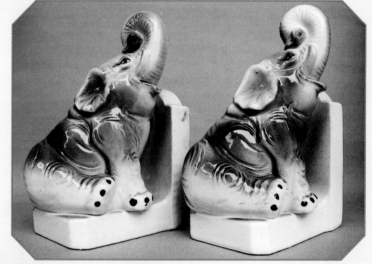

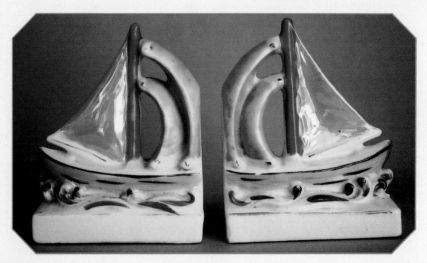

Plate 168. *Sailing ship bookends in multicolored luster and shiny glazes, 4½" tall, red mark #2, $28.00 – 48.00 pair.*

Bowls

Plate 169. *Geishas supporting a candy bowl in multicolored shiny glazes, 4½" tall, blue mark #52, $55.00 – 105.00.*

Plate 170. *Maruyama bowl with figural lady in polka dot pants and "MONTREAL CANADA" decal, 3½" tall, red mark #65, $20.00 – 35.00.*

Plate 171. *Clown bowl in multicolored shiny glazes, 10" long, black mark #2, $25.00 – 35.00.*

Plate 172. *Footed bowl in multicolored luster and shiny glazes, 7½" wide, red mark #56, $20.00 – 35.00.*

Plate 173. *Majolica-style footed bowl in multicolored shiny glazes, 4¼" tall, black mark #35, $20.00 – 35.00.*

Plate 174. *Rustic-style zigzag serving bowl in multicolored crackle glazes. reed handle, 11" wide, black mark #73a, $25.00 – 35.00.*

Plate 175. *Rustic bowls in multicolored crackle glazes, 5" wide, silver mark #170, $5.00 – 10.00 each.*

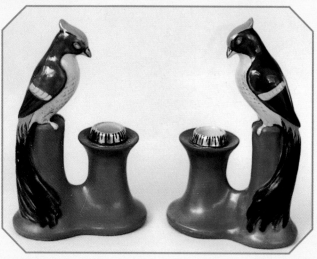

Plate 176. *Bird candleholders in multicolored semi-matte glazes, 5½" tall, black mark #1, $110.00 – 160.00 pair.*

Plate 177. *Candlestick holders with floral motif in multicolored shiny glazes, a pre-WWII set from the Akiyama store, 7¼" – 7½" tall, both black mark #2 with Japanese characters, $135.00 – 155.00 pair.*

Plate 178. *Candlestick holders in orange and multicolored shiny glazes, 5½" tall, black mark #52, $30.00 – 40.00 pair.*

Plate 179. *Majolica-style candlestick holders in multicolored shiny glazes, 3" tall, blind mark #1 with "KAWA," $20.00 – 35.00 pair.*

Plate 180. *Maruhon Ware majolica-style chamber stick in multicolored shiny glazes, 4" wide, black mark #35 with Japanese characters, single, as shown, $15.00 – 18.00; $40.00 – 65.00 pair.*

Plate 181. *Candleholders in multicolored luster glazes with pink candle cups, 4" wide, red mark #25, $40.00 – 65.00 pair.*

Plate 182. *Candleholders in multicolored luster glazes with butterfly motif, 4" wide, red mark #25, $40.00 – 65.00 pair.*

Plate 183. *Cambridge Glass Company candelabra #3400/638—but wait—it's not glass at all! It looks like Cambridge with an unusual enamel treatment, but it's ceramic, 6" tall, with multicolored shiny glazes and black mark #1, single, as shown, $10.00 – 15.00; $40.00 – 65.00 pair. This piece has been donated to the Cambridge Glass Museum in Cambridge, Ohio. The museum staff says it's not the first time they have seen a Cambridge piece reproduced in Made in Japan!*

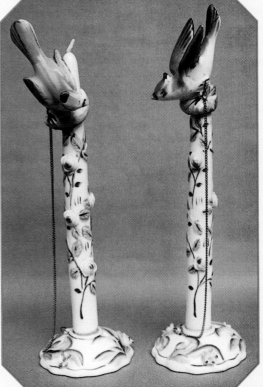

Plate 184. *Candleholders with attached bluebird candle climbers in multicolored shiny glazes, 3½" diameter, $15.00 – 25.00 pair; ceramic candles with rosebud decoration in multicolored shiny glazes, 10" tall, silver label obscured except for "JAPAN," $10.00 – 15.00 pair.*

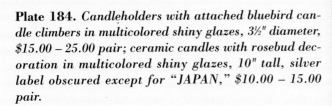

Cigarette and Tobacco Items

Plate 185. *Sheik cigarette set in multicolored shiny glazes, ashtrays have card suits, 5½" tall, blue mark #1, $50.00 – 75.00 with complete set of four ashtrays.*

Plate 186. *Clown with snuffers ashtray in multicolored shiny and semi-matte glazes, 5¼" tall, blue mark #1, $40.00 – 55.00.*

Plate 187. *Indian ashtray or ring tray in multicolored luster glazes, 4½" tall, black mark #56, $45.00 – 75.00.*

Plate 188. *Set of four clown card suit ashtrays in multicolored luster and shiny glazes, 1½" tall, (a and b) red mark #1, (c and d) red mark #32, $45.00 – 65.00 set.*

Plate 189. *Set of four card suit ashtrays in multicolored luster and shiny glazes, all 3" tall, (a) black mark #2, (b and c) black mark #1, (d) black mark #38, $45.00 – 65.00 set.*

Plate 190. *Set of four riding to hounds ashtrays in multicolored luster and shiny glazes, all 1½" tall, all red mark #1, $55.00 – 75.00 set.*

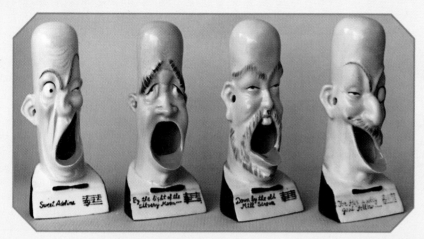

Plate 191. *Barbershop quartet "smoker" ashtray set in multicolored shiny and semi-matte glazes, 5" tall, label #60, $75.00 – 125.00 set. (These are copies of a German set. The Germans have incised numbers. These are also found with the "Occupied" or "Made in Occupied Japan" marks for about the same price.)*

Plate 192. *Bisque skeleton ashtray with attached legs and match holder in multicolored matte glazes, 3" tall, black mark #1, $65.00 – 85.00.*

Plate 193. *Two canoe-style ashtrays in multicolored luster and shiny glazes: (left) Cat, 1½" tall, red mark #1; Indian, 2" tall, $18.00 – 28.00 each.*

Plate 194. *Elephant on canoe ashtray in multicolored luster glazes, 1" tall, red mark #1, $18.00 – 28.00.*

Plate 195. *Calico elephant ashtray in multicolored shiny glazes, 4½" tall, black mark #1, $20.00 – 35.00.*

Plate 196. *Two monkey ashtrays in multicolored luster glazes: (left) Pair of monkeys with snuffers, 2½" tall, red mark #1; (right) Monkey with hat, 2½" tall, red mark #1, $30.00 – 45.00 each.*

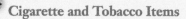

Plate 197. *Three Little Pigs ashtray in multicolored luster and shiny glazes, 4" wide, red mark #1, and blind mark #1 with "© Walt Disney," $175.00 – 250.00.*

Plate 198. *Dog and dish ashtray in multicolored luster and shiny glazes, 2½" tall, black mark #1, and blind mark #1, $20.00 – 30.00.*

Plate 199. *Dog and doghouse ashtray with snuffers in multicolored luster and shiny glazes, 2¼" tall, red mark #1, $20.00 – $30.00.*

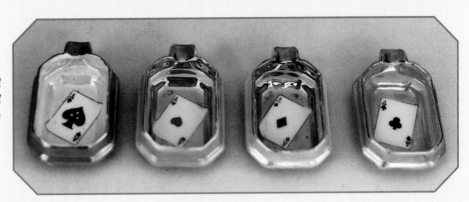

Plate 200. *Set of stacking card suit ashtrays in multicolored luster glazes, 3" long, red mark #50, $25.00 – 45.00 set.*

Plate 201. *Set of Noritake card suit ashtrays with scenic and floral motifs in multicolored shiny glazes, 2¾" – 3¼" wide, red mark #53, $65.00 – 95.00 set.*

Plate 202. *Trico ashtray in multicolored shiny glazes, 4½" wide, red mark #12, $20.00 – 25.00.*

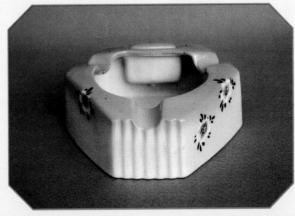

Plate 203. *Ashtray with cigarette holder in blue shiny glaze with majolica floral motif in the style of Coors Rosebud ware, 3" tall, black mark #2, $20.00 – 35.00.*

Plate 204. *Ashtray with match holder in multi-colored shiny glazes in the style of Coors Rosebud ware, 2¾" tall, black mark #1, $20.00 – 35.00.*

Plate 205. *Cigarette or playing card holder in maroon shiny glaze with sunbonnet girl motif, 4" tall, black mark #1, $20.00 – 35.00.*

Plate 206. *Two naughty bisque ashtrays with match holders: (left) inscribed "WHAT A BUST VANCOUVER WASH," 3¾" tall, red mark #1, $30.00 – 40.00; (right) inscribed "ON THE BUST," 4½" tall, black mark #2, $30.00 – 40.00.*

Plate 207. *Moriyama calico elephant lidded ashtray with cigarette and match panniers in multicolored shiny glazes, 5¾" tall, black mark #30, $30.00 – 45.00.*

Plate 208. *Noritake diamond card suit ashtray with pipe match holder in multicolored shiny glazes, green mark #53, 5¼" wide, $100.00 – 150.00.*

Plate 209. *Cigarette and match holder with bamboo-style handle in yellow and green shiny glazes, 4¼" tall, no mark, $20.00 – 35.00.*

Plate 210. *Two cigarette holders: (left) elephant with cigarette panniers and ashtray (shown in catalog on page 12 of this book) in multicolored luster and shiny glazes, 4¼" tall, red mark #1, $40.00 – 55.00; (right) bisque elephant with cigarette panniers in multicolored matte glazes, 4" tall, $30.00 – 45.00.*

Plate 211. *Two cigarette holders: (left) white elephant with cigarette holders in multicolored shiny glazes, 5¾" tall, black mark #1, $40.00 – 55.00; (right) green and yellow elephant with cigarette holders, 4½" tall, black mark #1, $30.00 – 45.00.*

Plate 212. *Lady seated on suitcase cigarette set in black and white shiny glazes on metal fitted base, lady 6½" tall, ashtrays, red mark #171, $165.00 – 200.00, complete with four stacking ashtrays. (This type of ware was also marked "Occupied Japan" or "Made in Occupied Japan.")*

Plate 213. *Lady with guitar cigarette set in multicolored luster and shiny glazes, 8¼" tall; base, red mark #24, ashtrays, black mark #1; $125.00 – 185.00, complete with four stacking ashtrays.*

Detail of lady with guitar.

Plate 214. *Maruyama Colonial lady cigarette set in multicolored shiny glazes, 6¼" tall, all red mark #65, $150.00 – 185.00, complete with four stacking ashtrays.*

Detail of Colonial lady.

Plate 215. *Satsuma-style cigarette set in multicolored matte and shiny glazes, 6" wide; base, red mark #1; cigarette holder, no mark, $50.00 – 75.00.*

Plate 216. *Robj-style cigarette box with match holder hat in multicolored shiny glazes, 7" tall, mark #1, $265.00 – 285.00.*

Plate 217. *Scottie dog cigarette set in multicolored shiny glazes, 4½" tall, all black mark #1, $50.00 – 60.00, complete with four stacking ashtrays.*

Plate 218. *Made in Japan revival Scottie dog cigarette set in black and white shiny glazes, incised "© 1981" and label #142 with "©1984," 6⅓" wide, $20.00 – 35.00 set.*

Plate 219. *Cottage cigarette set in multicolored shiny glazes, 4" tall, all black mark #3, $35.00 – 55.00, complete with four stacking ashtrays.*

Plate 220. *Maruyama Colonial cigarette set in multicolored shiny glazes, 4" wide, all red mark #65, and base blind mark #65, $20.00 – 35.00, complete with four stacking ashtrays.*

Detail of cigarette holder.

Plate 221. *Cigarette set with cherry blossom motif in multicolored luster glazes, pictured in a 1920s – 1930s Butler Brothers wholesale catalog for $.65 wholesale; $1.00 – $1.50 retail; tray, 7" wide, red mark #52, $50.00 – 75.00 set.*

Plate 222. *Majolica-style humidor with animal knob in multicolored shiny glazes, 7½" tall, black mark #1, $35.00 – 50.00.*

Plate 223. *Colonial gentleman in multicolored luster glazes, 6" tall, red mark #12a, $85.00 – 155.00.*

Plate 224. *Trico smoking set with card suit motif in multicolored luster and shiny glazes, 4½" tall, red mark #12, $55.00 – 75.00.*

Condiment Sets

Plate 225. *Popeye condiment set in multicolored luster and shiny glazes, 6½" wide, green mark #1, $625.00 – 650.00 set, with spoon.*

Plate 226. *Girl with flowers condiment set in multicolored shiny glazes, pictured in a 1920s – 1930s Butler Brothers wholesale catalog as part of an assortment of one dozen sets for $5.40 per dozen, 3¾" tall, all blind mark #1, $50.00 – 75.00 set, with spoon.*

Plate 227. *Chef condiment set in multicolored shiny glazes, 6" wide, mark #173 on tray only, $50.00 – 75.00 set, with spoon.*

Plate 228. *Cottage condiment set with gnomes in multicolored shiny glazes, note spoon with crook that resembles a little old chimney, 2¾" tall, all green mark #2, $30.00 – 45.00 set, with spoon.*

Plate 229. *Luster Native American fitted condiment set inscribed "Mohawk Trail," 2¾" tall, red mark #25, $50.00 – 75.00 set, with spoon.*

Plate 230. *Alligator condiment set in multicolored luster glazes, 4" tall, no mark, $120.00 – 135.00 set, with spoon.*

Plate 231. *Lobster condiment set in multicolored shiny glazes, salt and pepper, black mark #2, mustard pot and tray, black mark #1, $30.00 – 45.00 set, with spoon (This spoon may not be original.).*

Plate 232. *Lobster condiment set in orange semi-matte glaze, 7½" wide, salt and pepper, red mark #2, mustard pot and tray, red mark #66a, $35.00 – 55.00 set, with matching spoon, as shown.*

Plate 233. *Fish condiment set in pastel multicolored shiny glazes, 7¼" wide, salt and pepper, red mark #2, mustard pot and tray, red mark #66a, $35.00 – 55.00 set, with matching spoon, as shown.*

Plate 234. *Bonzo (a comic character dog whose greatest popularity was in England in the 1920s and 1930s) condiment set in multicolored luster glazes, tray, 7" wide salt and pepper, red mark #1; mustard pot and tray, red mark #28, $150.00 – 200.00 set, with spoon.*

Plate 235. *Rabbit condiment set in multicolored luster and shiny glazes, tray, 7" wide with green mark #25; mustard, green mark #1; salt, black mark #1; pepper, black mark #2; $35.00 – 55.00, set with matching red spoon.*

Plate 236. *Bird condiment set with cream and sugar set in multicolored luster glazes, tray, 7½" wide, all black mark #1, $125.00 – 150.00 set, with spoon.*

Plate 237. *Penguin oil and vinegar condiment set in multicolored shiny glazes, 7" tall, all black mark #1, $35.00 – 55.00 set.*

Plate 238. *Oil and vinegar condiment set with floral motif in multicolored luster glazes, tray, 7¼" wide; salt and pepper, black mark #1; cruets, mustard pot and tray, black mark #56; $35.00 – 55.00 set, with spoon.*

Plate 239. *Fitted Satsuma-style oil and vinegar condiment set in multicolored matte and shiny glazes, 6½" tall, salt and pepper, red mark #2; oil, vinegar, mustard pot and tray, red mark #21; $45.00 – 65.00 set, with matching brown, moriage-decorated spoon.*

Plate 240. *Oil and vinegar condiment set with stripe motif in multicolored shiny glazes, 6¾" tall, pepper, no mark; salt, red mark #1; mustard pot, tray, oil and vinegar, red mark #66d; $35.00 – 55.00 set, with spoon.*

Plate 241. *Oil and vinegar set on tray with floral motif in multicolored shiny glazes, tray, 9" wide, red mark #30b, $20.00 – 35.00 set.*

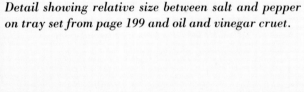

Detail showing relative size between salt and pepper on tray set from page 199 and oil and vinegar cruet.

Plate 242. *Mottoware condiment set in multicolored shiny glazes shown in the 1932 Sears Roebuck catalog for $.79, tray, 5¼" wide, black mark #30, $40.00 – 80.00 set, with matching brown-glazed spoon.*

Plate 243. *Corn condiment set in multicolored shiny glazes, tray 6¾" wide, all black mark #2, $20.00 – 35.00 set, with spoon (the spoon that originally came with this type of set is unglazed bisque).*

Plate 244. *Condiment set with floral motif in multicolored shiny glazes with reed handle, tray, 7½" wide, mustard pot and tray, red mark #25, salt and pepper, red mark #2; $20.00 – 35.00 set, with spoon.*

Plate 245. *Condiment set in multicolored luster glazes on a painted metal tray similar to the trays of the castor sets so popular in the earlier part of the twentieth century, tray, 5½" diameter, no mark; salt, pepper and mustard, black mark #1; $10.00 – 35.00 set (also offered with unpainted chrome trays).*

Plate 246. *Stacking condiment set in orange shiny glaze, 4" tall, silver foil "Made in Japan" label, $20.00 – 35.00 set, with spoon.*

Cream and Sugar Sets

Plate 247. *Shofu cream and sugar set with violet motif in multicolored shiny glazes, 3¾" tall, both green mark #10, $15.00 – 20.00 set.*

Plate 248 & 249. *Matching Shofu pieces to the cream and sugar set shown above, all with green mark #10: Salt and pepper, $8.00 – 10.00 pair; Butter dish with ceramic liner, $20.00 – 30.00; Bowl, $10.00 – 15.00.*

Plate 250. *Cowboy cream and sugar set in multicolored shiny glazes, 3" tall, red mark #1, $55.00 – 75.00 set.*

Plate 251. *Dogs with yellow eyes cream and sugar set in multicolored luster glazes, 6½" tall, black mark #1, $85.00 – 100.00.*

Plate 252. *Rabbit cream and sugar set in tan luster glaze, 4" tall, black mark #1, $35.00 – 55.00 set.*

Plate 253. *Cream and sugar set in multicolored luster glazes, tray, 7½" wide with black mark #52; cream and sugar, blind mark "Patent Applied For," $20.00 – 35.00 set.*

Plate 254. *Calico cream and sugar set in multicolored shiny glazes, tray, 8½" wide, all black mark #21, $15.00 – 25.00 set.*

Figurines

Plate 255. *Naughty bisque sailor figurine, 3½" tall, blind mark #1, $30.00 – 45.00.*

Plate 256. *Two small naughty bisque figurines with multicolored semi-matte glazes: (left) "That Old Feeling," 2½" tall, black mark #1; (right) "Goodbye Sweetheart," 3" tall, blind mark #1; $25.00 – 35.00 each.*

Plate 257. *Two soldiers in multicolored shiny glazes: (left) Drummer, 2" tall, red mark #2; (right) Marcher, 2" tall, red mark #2; $15.00 – 25.00 each.*

Plate 258. *Soldier trio in multicolored shiny glazes: (left) Rider, 3" tall, red mark #2; (right) Marchers, 2" tall, "Made In Occupied Japan;" $15.00 – 25.00 each.*

Plate 259. *World's Fair doll in purple and multicolored luster glazes inscribed "San Francisco Fair 1939," 4" tall, red mark #1, $50.00 – 75.00.*

Plate 260. *Bridal couple in multicolored shiny glazes, labels missing. $12.00 – 20.00 set.*

Plate 261. *Granny and gramps couple in multicolored shiny glazes, note background on gramps is same as on groom in photo shown on bottom of p. 128, blue and white "JAPAN" paper labels, $12.00 – 20.00 set.*

Plate 262. *Bisque football player, 5" tall, black mark #2, $18.00 – 28.00.*

Plate 263. *Barefoot fishing boy figurine in multicolored shiny glazes, 4¾" tall, blue mark #57, $35.00 – 40.00, with fish on line.*

Plate 264. *Monk musicians by INARCO in multicolored semi-matte glazes, 5¼" tall: (left) Violin, "E1609 ©1964;" Zither "E1609 ©1967;" $15.00 – 25.00 each.*

Plate 265. *Large Satsuma-style figure, 7" tall, red mark #1, $45.00 – 65.00.*

Plate 266. *Pair of bird figurines in multicolored shiny glazes, both red mark #1, $8.00 – 15.00 each.*

Plate 267. *Three figurines in multicolored glazes: (left) red and blue bird, red mark #1, $3.00 – 8.00; (center) yellow birds, 5¼" tall, label missing, $5.00 – 10.00; (right) bird on branch, 5" tall, blue lapel "JAPAN," $3.00 – 8.00.*

Plate 268. *Large Scottie dog figurine in multicolored shiny glazes, 10" tall, black mark #2, blind mark "H227A63," $35.00 – 50.00.*

Plate 269. *Small Scottie dog and orange cat joined figurine in shiny glazes, 3" tall, black mark #1, $15.00 – 25.00.*

Plate 270. *Boxer dog figurine in multicolored shiny glazes, 3½" tall, black mark #1, $10.00 – 18.00.*

Plate 271. *Dog figurine in multicolored shiny glazes, 4½" tall, black mark #1, $15.00 – 25.00.*

Plate 272. *Large snarling cat figurine in white shiny glaze on a tan clay body, 8" tall, blind mark #1, $30.00 – 45.00.*

Plate 273. *Cat on a shoe in multicolored luster and shiny glazes, 3¼" tall, red mark #2, $15.00 – 20.00.*

Plate 274. *Cat orchestra figurine in multicolored semi-matte glazes, 5" wide, red mark #1, $15.00 – 25.00.*

Plate 275. *Bunnies on base in multicolored luster glazes, 3¾" wide, black mark #1, blind mark #2, $15.00 – 25.00.*

Flower Bowls and Flower Frogs

Plate 276. *Circle of crabs flower or bulb bowl in multicolored luster and shiny glazes, 8½" diameter, $125.00 – 150.00.*

Plate 277. *Flower or bulb bowl with sprigged-on birds in multicolored luster glazes, 8" diameter, green mark #20, $70.00 – 85.00.*

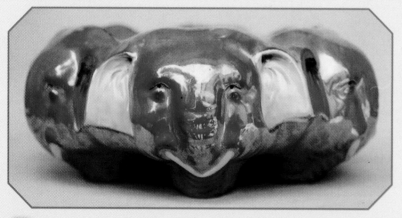

Plate 278. *Circle of elephants flower or bulb bowl in multicolored luster glazes, 9" diameter, red mark #1, $85.00 – 125.00.*

Plate 279. *Circle of birds flower or bulb bowl in multicolored luster glazes, 7" diameter, mark #56, $70.00 – 85.00.*

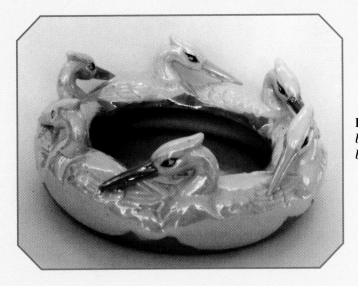

Plate 280. *Circle of egret-like birds flower or bulb bowl in multicolored luster glazes, 7½" diameter, black mark #25, $70.00 – 85.00.*

Plate 281. *Ducks chasing frogs flower or bulb bowl in multicolored luster glazes, 7½" wide, red mark #25, $70.00 – 85.00.*

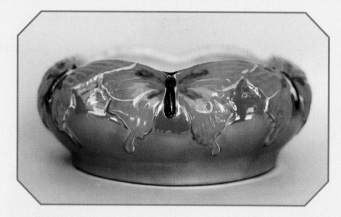

Plate 282. *Butterflies flower or bulb bowl in multicolored luster glazes, 8½" wide, red mark #25, $70.00 – 85.00.*

Plate 283. *Bird flower or bulb bowl with unattached frogs in multicolored luster glazes, 10" wide, black mark #1, $70.00 – 90.00, if complete with frogs.*

Plate 284. *Majolica-style console set in multicolored luster glazes, bowl, 9¼" diameter, black mark #1, $35.00 – 55.00 set.*

Plate 285. *Three flower or bulb bowls: 10¼" diameter, no mark; 6¾" diameter, blind mark #1; 3¾" diameter, blue mark #1; $15.00 – 30.00 each.*

Plate 286. *Awaji flower or bulb bowl in green shiny glaze, 11" diameter, blind mark #1, $30.00 – 65.00.*

Plate 287. *Flower or bulb bowl in multicolored luster and shiny glazes with rose motif, 6¾" diameter, black mark #1, $20.00 – 30.00.*

Plate 288. *Flower or bulb bowl in multicolored luster glazes with red flowers, 6¼" diameter, red mark #20, $20.00 – 35.00.*

Plate 289. *Majolica-style rectangular flower or bulb bowl in multicolored shiny glazes, 10¼" wide, black mark #1, $20.00 – 30.00.*

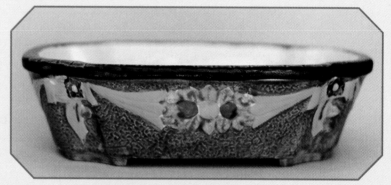

Plate 290. *Nude flower frog in white shiny glaze, 7" tall, blind mark #1 with "YANKOWARE," $30.00 – 45.00.*

Plate 291. *Pelican and fish flower frog in multicolored luster glazes, 4¾" tall, no mark, $75.00 – 85.00.*

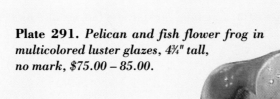

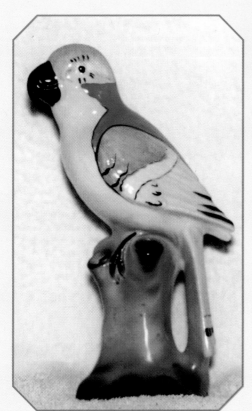

Plate 292. *Bird flower frog in multicolored luster and shiny glazes, 7" tall, mark #2, $50.00 – 75.00.*

Incense Burners

Plate 293. *Egyptian girl incense burner in multicolored shiny glazes, 5¾" tall, red mark #65, $65.00 – 95.00.*

Plate 294. *Japanese lady incense burner in multicolored luster glazes, 4" tall, red mark #1, $40.00 – 55.00.*

Plate 295. *Japanese lady with dog incense burner in multicolored luster glazes, 4¾" tall, black mark #52, $40.00 – 55.00 as pictured; $55.00 – 75.00, with domed cage that fits over the bowl.*

Plate 294. *Maruyama incense burner in multicolored shiny glazes, 3¾" tall, red mark #65, $20.00 – 30.00.*

Plate 297. *Buddha incense burner with match holder and slot for storing joss or incense in multicolored luster glazes, 5¼" long, black mark #25, $50.00 – 75.00.*

Plate 298. *Satsuma-style Buddha incense burner as shown in the 1929 Sears Roebuck catalog for $1.49, 5" tall, red mark #1, $55.00 – 65.00, as shown, with removable dome over the burner bowl; $20.00 – 35.00, without dome.*

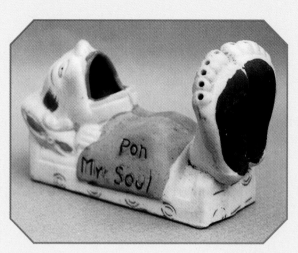

Plate 299. *Bisque "Pon My Soul" incense burner in multicolored matte glazes, 4¾" long, $20.00 – 35.00.*

Plate 300. *Large dog on book incense burner in multicolored shiny glazes, 7" tall, black mark #73a, $75.00 – 100.00.*

Plate 301. *Two cottage incense burners in multicolored semi-matte glazes with blind mark #1: (left) 4½" tall; (right) 4¼" tall; $20.00 – 35.00 each.*

Plate 302. *Cottage incense burner in multicolored semi-matte glazes, 4½" tall, blind marks #1 and #185, $20.00 – 35.00.*

Plate 303. *Cottage incense burner in multicolored semi-matte glazes, 3½" tall, blind mark #1, $20.00 – 35.00.*

Plate 304. *Pagoda incense burner in multicolored semi-matte glazes, 5" tall, blind marks #1 and #185, $20.00 – 35.00.*

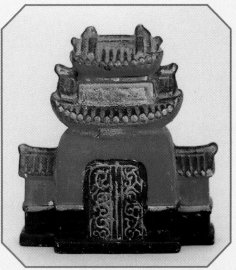

Plate 305. *Two boat incense burners in multicolored shiny glazes: (left) 4¼" tall, blind mark #1, red mark #38; (right) 4¼" tall, black mark #1; $20.00 – 30.00 each.*

Plate 306. *Incense burner with bird handles in multicolored luster glazes, 5¾" tall, red mark #25, $35.00 – 55.00, if complete with lid and inner cup as shown.*

Plate 307. *Small incense burner in orange and multicolored shiny glazes with moriage decoration, 3¼" tall, red mark #2, $12.00 – 18.00.*

Plate 308. *Grouping of Moriyama items showing relative sizes.*

Plate 309. *Moriyama biscuit barrel with reed handle, 7½" tall, black mark #30, $60.00 – 75.00.*

Plate 310. *Moriyama biscuit barrel, 7¾" tall with a handle span of 10", black mark #30a, $65.00 – 75.00.*

Plate 311. *Moriyama covered cake plate, 11" diameter, black mark #30a, $65.00 – 75.00.*

Plate 312. *Moriyama cereal bowl with under-plate, plate, 7¼" diameter, bowl, 5¼" diameter, $20.00 – 30.00 set.*

Plate 313. *Moriyama square range salt and pepper, 5" tall, mark #25, $25.00 – 45.00 pair.*

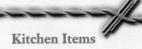

Plate 314. *Moriyama grouping: Salt and pepper set, 5" tall, black mark #30, $25.00 – 45.00 set; Salt box, 6½" tall, black mark #1, $65.00 – 85.00.*

Plate 315. *Moriyama cake plate pictured in the 1935 Sears Roebuck catalog as "Taisho Ware" for $.59, 12¼" diameter, black mark #1, $35.00 – 55.00; cake server, 10½" long, black mark #30, $35.00 – 55.00.*

Plate 316. *Moriyama grouping: cream and sugar set, 4½" – 5" tall, black mark #30, $35.00 – 55.00 set; drippings jar, 5" tall, black mark #30a, $35.00 – 55.00.*

Plate 317. *Moriyama handled tray, 10¼" wide, black mark #30a, $35.00 – 60.00.*

Plate 318. *Moriyama grouping: cup and saucer, black mark #30, $20.00 – 30.00 set; teapot, 6½" tall, black mark #30, $40.00 – 60.00.*

Plate 319. *Moriyama-style round range salt and pepper set, 4" tall, no mark, $25.00 – 35.00 set.*

Plate 320. *Majolica-style box on tray with square motif in multicolored shiny glazes, plate, 8½" diameter, mark #1, $25.00 – 35.00 set.*

Plate 321. *Blue covered canister or powder box in multicolored shiny glazes, 4¾" wide, blind mark #1, $15.00 – 25.00.*

Plate 322. *Triangle covered canister in multicolored shiny glazes (one section of a circled set), 4½" tall, mark #1, $15.00 – 25.00.*

Plate 323. *Triangle covered canister in multicolored shiny glazes (one section of a circled set), 2½" tall, mark #1, $15.00 – 25.00.*

Plate 324. *Cheese keeper in multicolored shiny glazes, 6¾" wide, red mark #175, $25.00 – 35.00.*

Plate 325. *Domino cream and sugar set in multicolored shiny glazes, named for the brand of sugar cubes that fit into the tray and circle the creamer like little rays, tray, 10½" handle span, no mark, $45.00 – 65.00.*

Kitchen Items

Plate 326. *Imitation Belleek grouping: Cream and sugar set, 3" – 4", green mark #1, $30.00 – 45.00 set; salt and pepper on tray set, tray black mark, "Made in Occupied Japan"; salt and pepper, black mark #2, $25.00 – 45.00. (This type of ware was still being pictured in the 1970s Norcrest catalogs).*

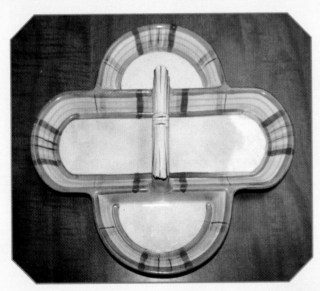

Plate 327. *Divided dish with bamboo-style handle in multicolored shiny glazes, 10½" wide, red mark #1, $35.00 – 45.00.*

Plate 328. *Egg cups in multicolored shiny glazes, 3½" tall, mark #29, $25.00 – 35.00 each.*

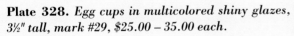

151

Plate 329. *Lunch box set in green and lavender shiny glazes, 6½" wide, bottom box only, black mark #72, $50.00 – 75.00 set.*

Plate 330. *Marmalade or jam pot on plate; plate, 5½" diameter, black mark #1, $25.00 – 35.00 set.*

Plate 331. *Match holder in multicolored shiny glazes, 7" tall, mark #73a, $25.00 – 45.00.*

Plate 332. *Corn napkin holder in multicolored shiny glazes, 5¼" tall, blue and white label "Made in Japan," $25.00 – 35.00.*

Plate 333. *Pancake or waffle batter set in multicolored shiny glazes, tray 10¾" wide, black mark #1, $55.00 – 75.00 set.*

Plate 334. *Salt box in multicolored shiny glazes, 5" tall, black mark #1, $30.00 – 45.00.*

Plate 335. *Salt box with cherry blossom motif in multicolored shiny glazes, 5" tall, mark #57b, $30.00 – 45.00.*

Plate 336. *Kitchen grouping in cobalt and multicolored shiny glaze, all mark #1: range salt and pepper set, 5" tall, mark #1, $25.00 – 45.00 set; drippings jar, 4" tall, $25.00 – 35.00.*

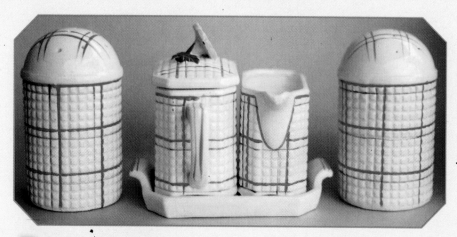

Plate 337. *Kitchen grouping with plaid motif in multicolored shiny glazes, all black mark #1: range salt and pepper, 5½" tall, $25.00 – 45.00 set; cream and sugar set with yellow flower finial, 6½" wide, $45.00 – 65.00 set.*

Plate 337. *Range salt and pepper with horizontal basketweave design in multicolored shiny glazes, 4½" tall, mark #1, $15.00 – 25.00 set.*

Plate 338. *Range salt and pepper with floral motif in multicolored shiny glazes, 4¾" tall, red mark #47, $15.00 – 25.00 set.*

Plate 339. *Range shaker set in cream and red shiny glazes, 4½" tall, red mark #50, $30.00 – 45.00 set.*

Plate 340. *Dutch figures spice set in multicolored shiny glazes, 11¾" wide, blue oval label "JAPAN," $55.00 – 75.00 set.*

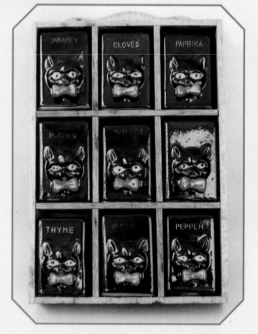

Plate 341. *Cat spice set in black shiny glaze on brown clay body, containers yellow mark #1, 11½" tall overall, $65.00 – 85.00.*

Plate 342. *Lazy Susan spice set in multicolored shiny glazes, 4" diameter, containers black mark #2, $20.00 – 35.00.*

Plate 343. *Book spice set with stripe motif in multicolored shiny glazes, 7½" wide, containers black mark #2, $25.00 – 35.00 set.*

Plate 344. *Book spice set with rooster motif in multicolored shiny glazes, 7½" wide, containers black mark #2, wooden rack label #176, $25.00 – 35.00 set.*

Plate 345. *Book spice set with chick motif in multicolored shiny glazes, 9" wide, containers black mark #2, $25.00 – 35.00 set.*

Plate 346. *Book spice set with windmill motif in multicolored shiny glazes, 7½" wide, containers black mark #2; wooden rack label #176, $25.00 – 35.00 set.*

Plate 347. *Book spice set with drawers in multicolored shiny glazes, 9½" wide, containers black mark #2; wooden rack label #176, $30.00 – 45.00 set.*

Plate 348. *Book figural chef spice set with blue neckerchiefs in multicolored shiny glazes, 8¼" wide, mark 183, $50.00 – 75.00 set.*

Plate 349. *Book figural chef spice set with bow ties in multicolored shiny glazes, 8¼" wide, containers black mark #2, $50.00 – 75.00 set.*

Plate 350. *Book figural chicken spice set in multicolored shiny glazes, 8" wide, containers black label with "JAPAN," $50.00 – 75.00 set.*

Plate 351. *Medieval figures spice set in multicolored shiny glazes, 5¼" wide, containers label #58, $25.00 – 35.00 set.*

Plate 352. *Square spice set with balloon motif in multicolored shiny glazes, 10" wide, containers label #57a, $25.00 – 35.00 set.*

Plate 353. *Square spice set with city scene motif in multicolored shiny glazes, 10" wide, containers black and white "JAPAN" label, $25.00 – 35.00 set.*

Plate 354. *Square spice set with oil and vinegar, with rooster motif in multicolored shiny glazes, 14" wide, black label with "JAPAN" on wooden rack, $25.00 – 35.00 set.*

Plate 355. *Square spice set with oil and vinegar, with duck motif in multicolored shiny glazes, 9½" wide, containers black label with "JAPAN," $25.00 – 35.00 set.*

Liquor Items

Plate 356. *Figural bottle stoppers in multicolored luster and shiny glazes: (left) Sea captain, 2¾" tall, black mark #1; (right) Mexican, 3" tall, blind mark #1; $10.00 – 20.00 each.*

Plate 357. *Figural rowboat bottle stopper in multicolored luster and shiny glazes, 2½" tall, no mark, $10.00 – 20.00.*

Plate 358. *Maw and Paw figural bottle stopper pourers in multicolored shiny glazes, 2½" – 2¾" tall, both black mark #2, $10.00 – 20.00 each.*

Plate 359. *Figural "Dead End Kid-style" bottle cork pourer in multicolored shiny glazes (cork is missing), 2¾" tall, red mark #2, $10.00 – 20.00.*

Plate 360. *Book decanters with cocktail recipes on sides in multicolored shiny glazes, wooden rack 7¾" wide, blue and white label "JAPAN," $40.00 – 55.00 set, if complete with ceramic stoppers.*

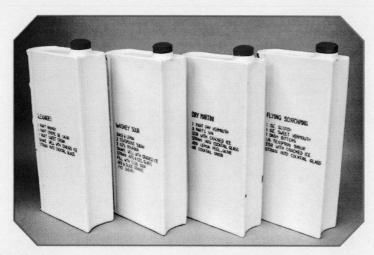

Detail of cocktail recipes.

Plate 361. *Bellhop decanter with shots in multicolored shiny glazes, decanter 11" tall, black mark #1; shots, no mark, $200.00 – 250.00, if complete with six shots.*

Plate 362. *Never on Sunday liquor set in brown shiny glaze over red clay body, decanter, 9¾" tall, label #59, $20.00 – 35.00 set.*

Plate 363. *Camera decanter in black shiny glaze over brown clay body, 8¾" tall, red and gold label "JAPAN," $15.00 – 20.00.*

Plate 364. *Colonial decanter or perfume bottle in multicolored shiny glazes with moriage accents, 7¾" tall, red mark #1, $20.00 – 35.00.*

Plate 365. *Figural decanter in multicolored shiny glazes, 6¼" tall, red mark #2, $20.00 – 35.00.*

Plate 366. *Rye dog decanter in multicolored shiny glazes, 10¼" tall, black and white label "JAPAN," $15.00 – 25.00.*

Plate 367. *Moriyama dog decanter in multicolored shiny glazes, 5½" tall, black mark #30, $15.00 – 25.00.*

Plate 368. *Polka dotted cat rye decanter with six shots in multicolored shiny glazes, decanter 7¾" tall with black and white label "JAPAN," shots black mark #2, $30.00 – 45.00 set.*

Plate 369. *Camel decanter set with scenic motif in multicolored shiny glazes, tray, 6½" wide, red mark #25, $80.00 – 105.00 as pictured; $175.00 – 195.00, complete with six or eight shots.*

Plate 370. *"Just a Little Nip" flask in multicolored luster glazes, 4½" tall, red mark #2, $50.00 – 75.00, with ceramic stopper.*

Plate 371. *Two figural flasks: (left) Bisque "Life Preserver" in multicolored semi-matte glazes, 4¾" tall, black mark #38, $95.00 – 150.00, with ceramic stopper; (right) Maruyama "Just a Little Nip/Souvenir of Hollywood, Calif." Bellhop in multicolored luster and shiny glazes, 4" tall, red mark #65, $50.00 – 75.00, if complete with ceramic stopper.*

Plate 372. *Bisque figural flask inscribed "Give Me a Wee O'Light" in multicolored shiny and semi-matte glazes, 4" tall, black mark #1 and blind mark #1, $50.00 – 75.00, with ceramic stopper.*

Plate 373. *Two flasks in multicolored luster and shiny glazes: (left) "ALL SCOTCH," 5½" tall, black mark #1; (right) 'FARM RELIEF," 5½" tall, black mark #1, $50.00 – 75.00 each, with ceramic stopper.*

Plate 374. *Uncle Sam flask inscribed "What We Want" in multicolored shiny glazes (not sure if his cork is a "marriage" or how he came originally as we have seen a drawing of it in a 1930s wholesale catalog where he does not appear to have a ceramic cork topper like this one does), 5" tall, black mark #1, $50.00 – 75.00.*

Plate 375. *Man with mirror flask inscribed "THE GOOD FELLOW WHO DRINKS WITH ME" in multicolored luster glazes, 4" tall, black mark #1, $50.00 – 75.00, with ceramic stopper.*

Plate 376. *Flask with drinking scene in multicolored shiny glazes, 4¼" tall, black mark #1, $50.00 – 75.00, with ceramic stopper.*

Plate 377. *Flask with golfer in multicolored luster and shiny glazes, 3½" tall, black mark #1, $50.00 – 75.00, with ceramic stopper.*

Plate 378. *Maruyama flask in multicolored luster and shiny glazes inscribed "NEVER DRINK WATER," 5¼" tall, red mark #65, $50.00 – 75.00, with ceramic stopper.*

Plate 379. *Maruyama dog liquor flask or perfume in multicolored luster and shiny glazes, 4¾" tall, red mark #65, $20.00 – 35.00.*

Plate 380. *Goldcastle flask inscribed "SOUVENIR OF ANAHEIM" with golf motif in multicolored luster glazes, (lid is a shot glass), 6" tall, black mark #43, $110.00 – 150.00.*

Mayonnaise Sets

Plate 381. *Mayonnaise set with cherry blossom motif in orange and multicolored shiny glazes, plate 6" diameter, blue mark #52, $15.00 – 25.00 set.*

Plate 382. *Mayonnaise set with scenic cartouche in multicolored luster glazes, a pre-WWII piece from the Akiyama store, plate 6" diameter, black mark #1, $20.00 – 40.00 set.*

Plate 383. *Noritake mayonnaise set in gold and white luster glazes, plate 5½" diameter with green mark #53, spoon and bowl no mark, $20.00 – 30.00 set.*

Plate 384. *Trico mayonnaise set in blue and multicolored shiny glazes, plate 6½" diameter, red mark #11, $20.00 – 35.00 set.*

Plate 385. *Trico mayonnaise set in multicolored shiny glazes with scenic motif, plate 6½" diameter, red mark #11, $20.00 – 35.00 set.*

Plate 386. *Lotus mayonnaise set in blue and multicolored shiny glazes, plate 6½" diameter, red mark #25 and #83, $15.00 – 25.00 set.*

Plate 387. *Lotus mayonnaise set in blue and tan luster glazes, plate 6½" diameter, all black mark #1, $15.00 – 25.00 set.*

Plate 388. *Goldcastle lotus mayonnaise set in pink and yellow luster glazes, plate 7" diameter, red mark #43, $15.00 – 25.00 set.*

Plate 389. *Figural Dutch people muffineer or berry sugar and creamer set in multicolored luster and shiny glazes, 5¾" tall, red mark #25, $85.00 – 125.00 set.*

Plate 390. *Figural Bonzo muffineer or berry sugar and creamer set in multicolored shiny glazes, black mark #24, 5¼" tall, $200.00 – 275.00 set.*

Plate 391. *Calico muffineer or berry sugar and creamer set in multicolored shiny glazes, 6¾" tall, black mark #1, $75.00 – 125.00 set.*

Plate 392. *Figural squash blossom muffineer or berry sugar and creamer set in orange and multicolored shiny glazes, 6¼" tall, black mark #1, $35.00 – 55.00 set.*

Plate 393. *Maruhon muffineer or berry sugar and creamer set with Majolica-style multicolored shiny glazes, 6" tall, black mark #35, $35.00 – 55.00 set.*

Plate 394. *Muffineer or berry sugar and creamer set with tan and multicolored luster and shiny glazes, 6" tall, red mark #24, $35.00 – 55.00 set.*

Plate 395. *Muffineer or berry sugar and creamer set with bamboo motif in black and tan shiny glazes, 7" tall, black mark #1, $35.00 – 55.00 set.*

Plate 396. *Muffineer or berry sugar and creamer set with floral motif in black and tan shiny glazes, 7" tall, black mark #1, $35.00 – 55.00 set.*

Plate 397. *Trico muffineer or berry sugar and creamer set with yellow floral motif in multicolored luster and shiny glazes, 6¾" tall, mark #11, $35.00 – 55.00 set.*

Plate 398. *Noritake muffineer or berry sugar and creamer set in blue and multicolored shiny glazes, 7" tall, red mark #53, $45.00 – 65.00 set.*

Plate 399. *Noritake muffineer or berry sugar and creamer set in multicolored shiny glazes, 6.5" tall, Red Mark #53 with "ROSEARA, U.S. DESIGN PAT APPLIED FOR," $45.00 – $65.00 set.*

Plate 400. *Noritake muffineer or berry sugar and creamer set with cottage motif in multicolored luster and shiny glazes, 6½" tall, red mark #53, $65.00 – 85.00 set.*

Plate 401. *Muffineer or berry sugar and creamer set in multicolored luster and shiny glazes with green oilspot decoration, 5¾" tall, red mark #25, $35.00 – 55.00 set.*

Plate 402. *Muffineer or berry sugar and creamer set with floral motif in multicolored luster glazes, 5¾" tall, red mark #25, $35.00 – 55.00 set.*

Plate 403. *Muffineer or berry sugar and creamer set with butterfly motif in white and multicolored luster and shiny glazes, 5¾" tall, red mark #25, $35.00 – 55.00 set.*

Nut Cups or Salt Dips

Plate 404. *Scottie nut cup or salt dip in black and white shiny glazes, 3" tall, red mark #2, $18.00 – 28.00.*

Plate 405. *Two nut cups or salt dips in multicolored shiny glazes, both, 3½" tall with black mark #29, $18.00 – 28.00 each.*

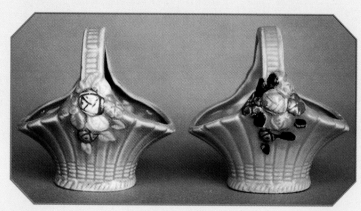

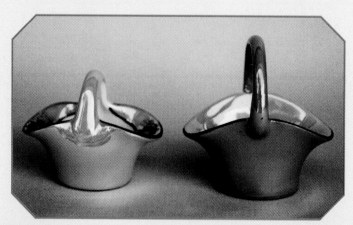

Plate 406. *Noritake nut cups or salt dips in multicolored luster glazes, both red mark #53: (left) 2¼" tall; (right) 1½" tall, $20.00 – 35.00 each.*

Plate 407. *Noritake nut cups or salt dips in multi-colored luster glazes, both, red mark #53: (left) Scenic motif, 1¾" tall; (right) Gold, 1½" tall, $20.00 – 35.00 each.*

Plate 408. *Nut cup or salt dip in gold and white shiny glazes, 1½" tall, red mark #2, $10.00 – 15.00.*

Plate 409. *Swan nut cup or salt dip in multicolored luster glazes, 2¾" tall, red mark #1, $8.00 – 15.00.*

Plate 410. *Pincushion with half doll in multicolored shiny glazes, 4½" tall overall, black mark #1, $20.00 – 35.00.*

Plate 411. *Pincushion with half doll and ceramic feet in multicolored luster and shiny glazes, 5" tall overall, red mark #1, $20.00 – 35.00.*

Plate 412. *Half doll for a pincushion in multicolored shiny glazes, 3¾" tall, black mark #2, $20.00 – 35.00.*

Plate 413. *Spanish lady pincushion in multicolored luster and shiny glazes, 4½" tall, black mark #1, $18.00 – 28.00.*

Plate 414. *Clown pincushion in multi-colored shiny glazes, 3" tall overall, black mark #2, $18.00 – 28.00.*

Plate 415. *Dutch girl pincushion with thimble in multicolored luster and shiny glazes, 3½" tall, red mark #1, $35.00 – 45.00.*

Plate 416. *African child pincushion in multicolored luster and shiny glazes, 2¾" tall, black mark #2, $50.00 – 75.00.*

Plate 417. *Three pincushions in multicolored luster and shiny glazes: (left) Long-legged man, 2¾" tall, red mark #1 and blind mark #1, $20.00 – 30.00; (center) Man with bird on his head, 3½" tall, blue mark #1 and blind mark #1, $20.00 – 30.00; (right) seated boy, 2¾" tall, red mark #1 and blind mark #1, $20.00 – 30.00.*

Plate 418. *Two pincushions in multicolored luster and shiny glazes: (left) pirate, 2½" tall, red mark #2; (right) cat, 2½" tall, black mark #2, $18.00 – 28.00 each.*

Plate 419. *Sailor boy pincushion in multicolored shiny glazes, 2¼" tall, red mark #1, $20.00 – 30.00.*

Plate 420. *Black cat pincushion in multicolored semi-matte glazes, 2" tall, red mark #2, $18.00 – 28.00.*

Plate 421. *Dog and cart pincushion in multicolored shiny glazes, 3¼" tall, red mark #1, $18.00 – 28.00.*

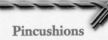

Plate 422. *Monkey pincushion in multicolored luster and shiny glazes, 3¼" tall, black mark #1, $20.00 – 35.00.*

Plate 423. *Dog driving bus pincushion in multicolored shiny glazes, 2¼" tall, red mark #1, $18.00 – 28.00.*

Plate 424. *Duck pincushion in multicolored luster glazes, 3½" tall, red mark #1, $20.00 – 30.00.*

Plate 425. *Stagecoach pincushion in multicolored shiny glazes, 4¼" wide, black mark #1, $18.00 – 28.00.*

Planters and Cache Pots

Plate 426. *Large boy with top hat cache pot in multi-colored shiny glazes, 7" tall, black mark #1, $20.00 – 35.00.*

Plate 427. *Majolica-style Dutch girl cache pot in multicolored shiny glazes, 5½" tall, black mark #1, $25.00 – 40.00.*

Plate 428. *Dutch boy and girl cache pot in green and white shiny glazes, 4" tall, red mark #1, $12.00 – 20.00.*

Plate 429. *Musical boy and girl cache pot in green and white shiny glazes, 4" tall, red mark #1, $12.00 – 20.00.*

Plate 430. *Mexican with guitar cache pot in multicolored shiny glazes, 3¼" tall, red mark #1, $12.00 – 20.00.*

Plate 431. *Two cache pots: (left) Siesta in multicolored matte glazes, 2½" tall, black mark #2, $8.00 – 15.00; (right) Native American in multicolored luster and shiny glazes, 4" tall, red mark #1, $20.00 – 35.00.*

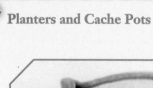

Plate 432. *Gnome cache pot in multicolored shiny glazes, 4½" tall, black mark #2, $12.00 – 20.00.*

Plate 433. *Majolica-style bird and worm cache pot in multicolored shiny glazes, 6" tall, black mark #2, $18.00 – 28.00.*

Plate 434. *Maruyama bird cache pot (note resemblance to glazing on Czech ceramics such as the wall pocket on page 16 of this book) in multicolored semi-matte glazes, 4½" tall, black mark #65, $18.00 – 28.00.*

Plate 435. *Two fowl cache pots: (left) rooster in blue and multicolored semi-matte glazes, 3¾" tall, black mark #2, $12.00 – 20.00; (right) bird on nest in multicolored shiny glazes, 4¼" tall, black mark #1, $10.00 – 18.00.*

Plate 436. *Bird and buggy cache pot in multicolored luster and shiny glazes, 3" tall, red mark #89, $12.00 – 20.00.*

Plate 437. *Two treehouse cache pots in multicolored shiny glazes: (left) squirrel, 4" tall, black mark #2; (right) bird, 4" tall, black mark #1; $12.00 – 20.00 each.*

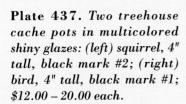

Plate 438. *Dog cache pot in multicolored shiny glazes, 7¼" long, black mark #1, $12.00 – 20.00.*

Plate 439. *Scottie cache pot in black and white shiny glazes, 5" tall, green mark #68, $12.00 – 20.00.*

Plate 440. *Two donkey cache pots in multicolored shiny glazes, both black mark #1: (left) 4" tall; (right) 3¾" tall, $12.00 – 20.00 each.*

Plate 441. *Large elephant cache pot in multicolored shiny glazes, 6¼" tall, black mark #2, $15.00 – 25.00.*

Plate 442. *Two elephant cache pots in multicolored crackle glazes: (left) 7¼" tall, black mark #1, $18.00 – 28.00; (right) 5" tall, black mark #24, $15.00 – 25.00.*

Plate 443. *Large swan cache pot in green shiny glaze, 12½" long, blind mark #1, $18.00 – 28.00.*

Plate 444. *Cache pot with drip glaze, 3½" tall, no mark, $20.00 – 25.00.*

Plate 445. *Jardinière in the style of Rookwood Pottery in multicolored shiny glazes, 5½" tall, blind mark #1, $30.00 – 45.00.*

Plate 446. *Majolica-style cache pot with fruit motif in multicolored shiny glazes, 5½" tall, black mark #1, $12.00 – 20.00.*

Plate 447. *Majolica-style cache pots in multicolored shiny glazes: (left) 3½", black mark #1; (right) 3½" tall, black mark #29; $10.00 – 18.00 each.*

Plate 448. *Card suit planter in white shiny glaze with suits in pink and blue, 3" tall, $15.00 – 25.00.*

189

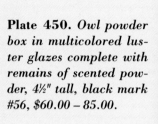

Plate 450. *Owl powder box in multicolored luster glazes complete with remains of scented powder, 4½" tall, black mark #56, $60.00 – 85.00.*

Plate 449. *Lady powder box in multicolored luster glazes, 3¾" tall, black mark #1 and blind mark #1, $65.00 – 85.00.*

Plate 451. *Small Awaji powder or cosmetic box in purple shiny glaze, 2" tall, no mark, $10.00 – 20.00.*

Plate 452. *Small footed powder or cosmetic box in tan and blue luster glazes, 2½" tall, black mark #115, $20.00 – 35.00.*

Plate 453. *Powder box in multicolored luster glazes, 5" tall, black mark #1, $35.00 – 55.00.*

Plate 454. *Stove salt and pepper with instant coffee container (Note: these were made in several styles and colors over the years, starting with separate shakers and gradually evolving to molded-in coffee pots that were not shakers, just decorations.), 5½" tall, label #177, $20.00 – 35.00 set, with original plastic spoon.*

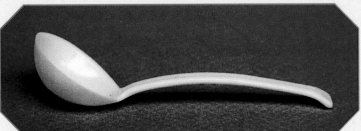

Detail of original plastic spoon.

Plate 455. *Popeye and Olive Oyl salt and pepper on tray set in multicolored shiny glazes, 3½" wide, salt and pepper no mark, base black mark #1, $85.00 – 125.00 set.*

Plate 456. *Japanese lady with lotus blossom salt and pepper set in multicolored luster and shiny glazes, 4", black mark #1, $40.00 – 60.00 set.*

Plate 457. *Porter salt and pepper set in multicolored shiny glazes, 5¼" tall, red and gold label, "MADE IN JAPAN," $18.00 – 28.00 set.*

Plate 458. *Bellhop salt and pepper set in multicolored shiny glazes, 4" tall, black mark #2, $85.00 – 125.00 set.*

Plate 459. *Lady with hatbox salt and pepper set in multicolored shiny glazes, 5" tall, black mark #1, $85.00 – 125.00 set.*

Plate 460. *Native American nodder salt and pepper set in multicolored shiny glazes, 3¾" tall, base red mark #1, shakers blind stamped "PATENT TT," $75.00 – 125.00 set.*

Plate 461. *Kangaroo and joey salt and pepper set in multicolored shiny glazes, 4⅓" tall, salt and pepper red mark #2, base red mark #1, $25.00 – 35.00 set.*

Plate 462. *Gingham dog and calico cat salt and pepper set in multicolored shiny glazes, 3¼" tall, red mark #2, $15.00 – 20.00 set.*

Plate 463. *Birds and nests salt and pepper on tray set in multicolored shiny glazes, 3" tall, salt and pepper red mark #2, base black mark #1, $15.00 – 25.00 set.*

Plate 464. *Bird salt and pepper on tray set in multi-colored shiny glazes, 3¾" wide, salt and pepper black mark #1, tray black mark #2, $15.00 – 25.00 set.*

Plate 465. *Fish salt and pepper on tray set in multicolored shiny glazes, 4¾" wide, tray black mark #18, $15.00 – 25.00 set.*

Plate 466. *Bunny salt and pepper on tray set in multicolored shiny and semi-matte glazes, 5¼" wide, salt and pepper red mark #1, tray red mark #25, $30.00 – 45.00 set.*

Plate 467. *Sailboat and lighthouse salt and pepper on tray set in multicolored shiny glazes, 3¾" tall, all red mark #2, $20.00 – 30.00 set.*

Plate 468. *Cottages and windmill salt and pepper on tray set in multicolored shiny glazes, 2¾" tall, salt and pepper no mark, tray black mark #1, $15.00 – 25.00 set.*

Plate 469. *Egg salt and pepper on tray set in multicolored shiny glazes, 4" wide, black mark # 178, $15.00 – 25.00 set.*

Plate 470. *Yellow plaid egg salt and pepper on tray set in multicolored shiny glazes, 6" wide, black and white label "JAPAN," $15.00 – 25.00 set.*

Plate 471. *Humpty Dumpty salt and pepper on base set in multicolored shiny glazes, 4½" wide, no mark, $15.00 – 25.00 set.*

Plate 472. *Native American salt and pepper on tray set in multicolored shiny glazes, 4½" wide, black mark #179, $15.00 – 25.00 set.*

Plate 473. *Cream and sugar-shaped salt and pepper on tray set in multicolored shiny glazes, 6½" wide, red mark #2, $15.00 – 25.00 set.*

Plate 474. *Teapot-shaped salt and pepper on tray set with stripe motif in multicolored shiny glazes, 5" wide, red mark #180, $15.00 – 25.00 set.*

Plate 475. *Cream and sugar-shaped salt and pepper on tray set in multicolored shiny glazes, 5½" wide, red mark #2, $15.00 – 25.00 set.*

Plate 476. *Geometric teapot-shaped salt and pepper on tray set in multicolored shiny glazes, 5" wide, black mark #1, $15.00 – 25.00 set.*

Plate 477. *Teapot-shaped salt and pepper on tray set in multicolored shiny glazes, 6" wide, red mark #50, $15.00 – 25.00 set.*

Plate 478. *One-piece Asian with lantern figural salt and pepper set in multicolored shiny glazes inscribed "CHINA TOWN SAN FRANCISCO" (back of lady is a shaker, and the lantern is also a shaker), 3½" tall, $45.00 – 65.00.*

A.

B.

C.

Plate 479. *Unusual tea set in that tumblers are included, in multicolored luster glazes: A.) Teapot, 6¼" tall with black mark #28; B.) Cup, saucer and tumbler; C.) Cream and sugar and plate; service for four, $35.00 – 55.00.*

Plate 480. *Teapot and tile in multicolored luster glazes, 6½" tall, red mark #25, $35.00 – 55.00 set.*

Plate 481. *Late Taisho – early Showa period Satsuma teapot from the 1920s, 6" tall, mark #181, $75.00 – 85.00.*

Plate 482. *Satsuma cup and saucer from the 1920s, mark #181, $20.00 – 30.00.*

Plate 483. *Teapot with hot water pot on tray in red and white shiny glazes, tray 10¾" wide, all red mark #47, $45.00 – 65.00 set.*

Plate 484. *Native American teapot in multicolored shiny glazes, 5½" tall, black mark #1, $35.00 – 55.00.*

Detail of Drip-o-lator insert and lid.

Plate 485. *Drip-o-lator coffee pot in multicolored luster and shiny glazes, 11½" tall, red mark #1, $35.00 – 55.00.*

A BIG CUT
in the Jobbing Price of
Tooth Brushes

Frankly, we ordered too many tooth brushes from Japan so that we will let a few thousand gross go at a big reduction in price. We would get out of the tooth brush business if we had to do this regularly, but this is your opportunity to buy at low prices that surely will not prevail in the near future.

Anticipate your wants - BUY NOW, later they will cost more. Look over the following list and send us your order for a sample box each of such numbers as you think will be interesting so that you may examine the quality, style etc., and determine the size of your order. All bone handles. Packed half dozen to box.

Number	Description				Jobbers' Price	Special Sale Price
3324	4 Row		74 Holes		26.00	19.75
3325	4 Row		96 "	OPEN BACK	23.00	17.75
3333	4 Row Bristles		96 "	"	22.50	17.50
3337	4 " "		112 "	"	22.00	17.00
3342	4 " "		108 "	"	22.50	17.50
3349	4 " "		120 "		22.50	17.50
3353	4 " "		76 "		24.50	18.75
3355	4 " "		96 "		27.50	21.00
3358	4 " "		72 "		27.50	21.25
5355	4 " "		80 "		18.50	14.00
5356	4 " "		96 "		18.50	14.00
5368	4 " "		96 "	OPEN BACK	21.50	16.50
5370	4 " "		96 "	"	23.75	18.25
5373	4 " "		88 "	"	21.50	16.50
5374	4 " "		76 "	PERFORATED BACK	23.75	18.25
5376	4 " "		96 "	"	21.50	16.50
5377	4 " "		112 "	"	26.75	20.50
5378	4 " "		62 "		22.50	17.50
5381	4 " "		96 "	OPEN BACK	25.00	19.50
5382	4 " "		88 "		25.00	19.50
5383	4 " "		112 "		23.50	17.75
5388	4 " "		54 "	PERFORATED BACK	25.50	19.75
5389	4 " "		104 "	"	21.00	16.50
5390	4 " "		72 "		24.25	18.75
5392	4 " "		108 "		26.50	20.25
5394	4 " "		80 "		31.50	25.00
5395	4 " "		68 "		36.75	28.50

Terms 2% 10 days, Net 30 days, f.o.b. New York

YANO & JOKO
440 Fourth Avenue - - - - New York

Plate 486. *Bellhop toothbrush holder in multicolored shiny glazes, 5¾" tall, $135.00 – 155.00.*

Plate 487. *Two bellhop toothbrush holders in multicolored luster glazes shown in the 1933 Sears Roebuck catalog for $.25 each including toothbrush: (left) 6¾" tall, red mark #1; (right) 6¾" tall, red mark #11; $95.00 – 135.00 each.*

Plate 488. *Two toothbrush holder girls in multicolored luster and shiny glazes, 3¼" tall, blind mark #1, $85.00 – 125.00 each.*

Plate 489. *Dutch boy toothbrush holder in multicolored luster and shiny glazes, 4¾" tall, black mark #1, $95.00 – 135.00.*

Plate 490. *Two men with hats toothbrush holders in multicolored luster and shiny glazes, both with red mark #1: (left) derby hat, 5" tall; (right) top hat with inscription "TACOMA," 5½" tall; $95.00 – 135.00 each.*

Plate 491. *Two boy toothbrush holders in multicolored luster and shiny glazes, both black mark #1: (left) post box, 4¼" tall; (right) 4¾" tall; $95.00 – 135.00 each.*

Plate 492. *Set of three nursery rhyme toothbrush holders in multicolored shiny glazes: butcher, 5¼" tall, red mark #1; baker, 5¼" tall, red mark #1; candlestick maker, 5" tall, red mark #44; $100.00 – 150.00 each.*

Plate 493. *Two toothbrush holders in multicolored shiny glazes: (left) boy with violin, 5" tall, red mark #14; (right) Little Red Riding Hood with label on back inscribed "SOUVENIR OF ASHTABULA," 4½" tall, black mark #1; $95.00 – 135.00 each.*

Plate 494. *Pair of imitation Hummel toothbrush holders in multicolored shiny glazes, 7" tall, both black mark #1, $95.00 – 135.00 each.*

Plate 495. *Musician toothbrush holders in multicolored luster and shiny glazes, 4¼" – 4½" tall, all black mark #1, $95.00 – 135.00 each.*

Plate 496. *Two bisque comic character toothbrush holders with multicolored cold paint: (left) 4", black mark #2 and inscribed "UNCLE WALT and SKEEZIX © FAS, S1554"; (right) Little Orphan Annie and Sandy, 3¾" tall, black mark #1 and inscribed "S691, © FAMOUS ARTISTS SYNDICATE"; $175.00 – 250.00 each.*

Plate 497. *Two bisque comic character toothbrush holders with multicolored cold paint: (left) 4" tall, inscribed "THREE LITTLE PIGS" on front and "S155 © WALT DISNEY" with blind mark #1 on back, $175.00 – 250.00; Donald Duck, 5¼" tall, blind mark #1 and inscribed "© WALT DISNEY" on back, $300.00 – 325.00.*

Plate 499. *Crow toothbrush holder in multicolored luster and shiny glazes, 5¾" tall, red mark #56, $95.00 – 135.00.*

Plate 498. *Two toothbrush holders in multicolored shiny glazes: (left) Elephant, 3¾" tall, blind mark #1 with "Yanko Made; (right) Soccer player, 4¾" tall, no mark; $95.00 – 135.00 each.*

Research has shown these to have been sold as both toothbrush holders and toothpick holders.

Plate 500. *(Left to right) Cats, 3" tall; monkeys 2¾" tall; dogs, 2¾" tall; all red mark #1; $20.00 – 35.00 each.*

Plate 501. *(Left) Elephants, 2½", black mark #2; (right) bears, 2¼" tall, black mark #1 and blind mark #1; $20.00 – 35.00 each.*

Plate 502. *Toothbrush holder in multicolored shiny glazes inscribed "THE THREE BEARS," 5" tall, black mark #2 and blind mark #18, $125.00 – 150.00.*

Plate 503. *Bear toothbrush holder in multicolored shiny glazes, 5½" tall, blind mark #21 with Japanese characters, $95.00 – 135.00.*

Plate 504. *(Left) Bird toothbrush holder in multicolored shiny glazes, 3¼" tall, red mark #1; (right) penguin, 5½" tall, black mark #2, $95.00 – 135.00 each.*

Plate 505. *(Left) Duck triple toothbrush holder in white and gold shiny glazes, 5¾" tall, blue mark #44; (right) cow in multicolored shiny glazes, 3½" tall, black mark #1; $95.00 – 135.00 each.*

Plate 506. *Three toothbrush holders in multicolored luster glazes: (left) bull, 4¼" tall, black mark #43,; (center) baby bull, 3½" tall, red mark #1; (right) Bonzo-like dog, 4¼" tall, red mark #43; $85.00 – 125.00 each.*

Plate 507. *Two cat toothbrush holders in multicolored luster glazes: (left) 4" tall, black mark #1; (right) 4½" tall, red mark #43; $85.00 – 125.00 each.*

Plate 508. *Two Goldcastle Scottie toothbrush holders in multicolored shiny glazes: (left) card game, 4¼" tall, red mark #44; (right) with pouch, 6½" tall, red mark #43; $95.00 – 135.00 each.*

Plate 509. *Two calico toothbrush holders: (left) Goldcastle grinning dog, 4" tall, red mark #43; Tall dog, 5" tm black mark #1; $95.00 – 135.00 each.*

Plate 510. *Two calico cat toothbrush holders: (left) 4½" tall, red mark #1; (right) 5¾" tall, black mark #1; $95.00 – 135.00 each.*

Plate 511. *Two Bonzo toothbrush holders in multicolored shiny glazes: (left) 5½" tall, blind mark #2 with "© The Hinode;" (right) 5½" tall, shown in the Spring 1932 Sears Roebuck catalog as "Taisho Ware" for $.29, complete with toothbrush; $200.00 – 300.00 each.*

Plate 512. *Bugs Bunny-like bank in multicolored shiny glazes, 4¾" tall, black mark #57c, $25.00 – 45.00.*

Plate 513. *Ship bank in multicolored shiny glazes with "FOR MY TRIP" incised on the lower right sail, 5¾" tall, red mark #2, $20.00 – 35.00.*

Plate 514. *Figural dog clothes brush in multicolored shiny glazes with original box, 8" tall, brush, red mark #1, box black mark #1, $50.00 – 70.00, with box.*

Plate 515. *Calendar in multicolored luster and shiny glazes with day/date/month cards, 2¾" tall, black mark #2, $35.00 – 55.00, with complete set of cards ($15.00 – 25.00, without).*

Plate 516. *Golf dresser caddy in multicolored shiny glazes, 6" tall, label #182, $15.00 – 20.00.*

Plate 517. *Goldcastle swan candy box in multicolored luster glazes, 5¼" tall, red mark #43, $35.00 – 45.00.*

Plate 518. *Frog cocktail pick holder in multicolored shiny glazes, $35.00 – 45.00.*

Plate 519. *Bellhop egg timer in multicolored shiny glazes, 2¾" tall, blind mark #1, $50.00 – 75.00.*

Plate 520. *Veggie man egg timer in multicolored semi-matte glazes, 4" tall, black mark #1, $50.00 – 75.00.*

Plate 521. *Three egg timers in multicolored shiny glazes: (left) colonial lady, 4¾" tall, black mark #1 and blind mark #1; calico rabbit, 3¼" tall, black mark #2; chef, 3¾" tall, black mark #3; $50.00 – 75.00 each.*

Plate 522. *Child's feeding bowl in multicolored luster and shiny glazes, 5" diameter, red mark #25, $35.00 – 50.00.*

Plate 523. *Lamp with Colonial couple in multicolored shiny glazes, 6¾" tall, $15.00 – 25.00.*

Plate 524. *Elephant lamp in multicolored luster and shiny glazes, 7" tall to beginning of socket, mark covered, $35.00 – 55.00.*

Plate 525. *Lemon server in multicolored luster glazes, 6" diameter, red mark #66b, $18.00 – 28.00.*

Plate 526. *Lemon server with bird handle in orange and white shiny glazes, 6" wide, red mark #50, $18.00 – 28.00.*

Plate 527. *Lemon server with Mexican motif in multicolored shiny glazes, 5½" wide, red mark #47, $18.00 – 28.00.*

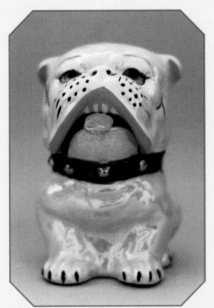

Plate 528. *Figural dog marmalade with ladle tongue shown in the 1932 Sears Roebuck catalog with the brand name "Taisho Ware" with underplate in assorted colors for $.19 per set, 5" tall, as shown with ladle, $50.00 – 75.00; with underplate, $65.00 – 125.00.*

Plate 529. *Girl and boy napkin rings in multicolored shiny glazes, 4¼" tall, boy, black mark #2, girl, black mark #1, $25.00 – 35.00 each.*

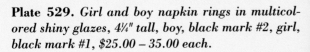

Plate 530. *Boy napkin ring in orange and multi-colored shiny glazes, Mark #18, $25.00 – 35.00.*

Plate 531. *Colonial lady napkin ring in multi-colored shiny glazes, 4" tall, red mark #1, $25.00 – 35.00.*

Plate 532. *Perfume set in multicolored luster and shiny glazes with metal holder, 6½" tall, bottles red mark #25, holder blind mark #1, $65.00 – 95.00 set.*

Plate 533. *Rabbit perfume in multicolored luster glazes, 3½" tall, red mark #25, $50.00 – 75.00.*

Plate 534. *Majolica-style rooster pitcher in multicolored shiny glazes, 5" tall, blue mark #2, $15.00 – 25.00.*

Plate 535. *Rooster pitcher in multicolored luster glazes, 3½" tall, red mark #2, $15.00 – 25.00.*

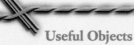

Plate 536. *Pair of wall plaques in multicolored, cold-painted glazes, 6" and 5½" tall, both black mark #23 with label "FW Woolworth $.29," $20.00 – 30.00 each.*

Plate 537. *Duck and penguin place card holders in multicolored luster and shiny glazes, 3¾" tall, black mark #2, $15.00 – 25.00 each.*

Plate 538. *Set of Commodore place card holders with flowers, 2" tall, label #39, $20.00 – 30.00 set with original box.*

Plate 539. *Spotted creature soap dish in green and yellow shiny glazes, 4¼" tall, blue mark #1, $15.00 – 25.00.*

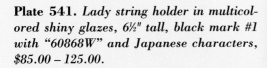

Plate 540. *Soap dish with tennis player in multicolored luster glazes, 3¾" tall, red mark #1 and blind mark #1, $50.00 – 75.00.*

Plate 541. *Lady string holder in multicolored shiny glazes, 6½" tall, black mark #1 with "60868W" and Japanese characters, $85.00 – 125.00.*

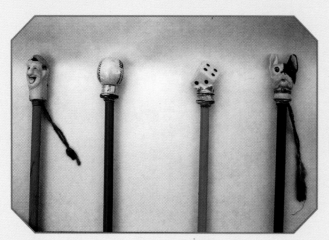

Plate 542. *Swagger sticks given as carnival prizes in multicolored luster and shiny glazes: From left to right: face, 2¼" tall, black mark #2, $55.00 – 75.00; baseball, 2" tall, black mark #2, $35.00 – 45.00; dice, 2" tall, blind mark #2, $35.00 – 45.00; dog, 2¼" tall, black mark #2 and blind mark #2, $35.00 – 45.00.*

Plate 543. *Clown thermometer in multicolored luster and shiny glazes, 4¾" tall, red mark #1, $45.00 – 65.00.*

Plate 544. *Teapot toothpick holder in green shiny glaze in original package, pot, 3¼" tall with blind mark #1, package "©1983 TRAVCO Brooklyn N.Y. 11203 Made in Japan," $5.00 – 10.00.*

Plate 545. *Dog toothpick holder in multicolored luster glazes, 3" tall, red mark #74, $20.00 – 35.00.*

Vases
Hanging

Plate 546. *Parrot hanging vase in multicolored luster glazes, black mark #1, $90.00 – 130.00.*

Plate 547. *Majolica-style floral hanging vase in multicolored shiny glazes, 6½" tall, black mark #80, $85.00 – 125.00.*

Plate 548. *Majolica-style hanging vase with floral motif in multicolored shiny glazes, 6½" tall, black mark #1, $85.00 – 125.00.*

Plate 549. *Hanging vase with bird motif and original chains in turquoise glaze, 4" tall, black mark #1, $90.00 – 130.00.*

Plate 550. *Turnip-shaped hanging vase in multicolored luster and shiny glazes, 5½" tall, red mark #25, $35.00 – 55.00.*

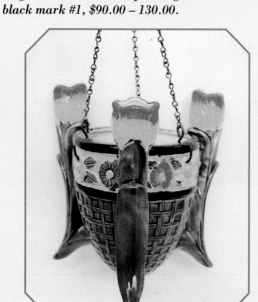

Plate 551. *Majolica-style hanging vase with attached bud vases and original chain in multicolored shiny glazes, 6½" tall, blind mark #1, $85.00 – 125.00.*

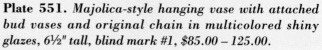

Plate 552. *Tokanabe hanging vase (Tokanabe was the name the Sears Roebuck catalog gave to this type of ware) in multicolored matte glazes, 4¾" tall, blind mark #1, $35.00 – 55.00.*

Plate 553. *Fukagawa vase with acanthus motif in blue and white shiny glazes, 6" tall, blue mark #186, $95.00 – 105.00.*

Plate 554. *Koransha vase with maple leaf motif in multicolored shiny glazes, 6" tall, blue mark #187, $75.00 – 85.00.*

Plate 555. *Early twentieth century art vase with floral motif in blue and white shiny glazes, 4¾" tall, no mark, $45.00 – 50.00.*

Plate 556. *Late nineteenth century art vase with hemp motif in blue and white shiny glazes, no mark, $75.00 – 85.00.*

Plate 557. *Tall, hand-thrown white vase with birds nesting in pines motif, in blue and white shiny glazes, 12" tall, no mark, $55.00 – 75.00.*

Plate 558. *Late Taisho – early Showa period small Satsuma cylinder vase from the 1920s. Small Satsuma cylinder vase, 5" tall, mark #188, $55.00 – 75.00.*

Plate 559. *Pair of late Meiji Satsuma vases in a scarce color, 6¼" tall, mark #189, $250.00 – 260.00 pair.*

Plate 560. *Chinese-style square vase in multicolored shiny glazes, 6" tall, no mark, $15.00 – 25.00.*

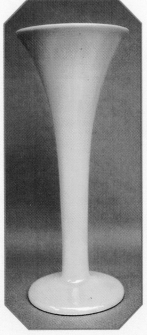

Plate 561. *Yellow trumpet vase, 9¾" tall, blind mark #2, $40.00 – 45.00.*

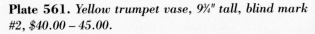

Plate 562. *Vase with multicolored Asian motif, 9" tall, mark obliterated, $160.00 – 180.00.*

Plate 563. *Vase with multicolored floral motif on gray crackle glaze, 8" tall, no mark, $175.00 – 195.00.*

Plate 564. *Vase with cherry blossom motif in multicolored shiny glazes, 6" tall, no mark, $160.00 – 180.00.*

Plate 565. *Vase with floral motif in white and multicolored shiny glazes, 7½" tall, black mark #73a, $35.00 – 55.00.*

Plate 566. *Small, late Victorian-style vase in green and yellow shiny glazes, 3⅓" tall, no mark, $30.00 – 45.00.*

Plate 567. *Vase with green shiny glaze, 7¼" tall, black mark #1, $20.00 – 35.00.*

Plate 568. *Arts & Crafts-style vase similar to Roseville's Monticello line of 1931 in multicolored shiny glazes, 5" tall, black mark #1, $30.00 – 40.00.*

Plate 569. *Pair of vases with lavender shiny glaze, 5½" tall, blind mark #149, $20.00 – 35.00 pair.*

Drip glaze vases similar to Roseville's Carnelian of the 1920s.

Plate 570. *Arts & Crafts-style vase in multicolored green glaze, 8" tall, blind mark #2, $100.00 – 125.00.*

Plate 571. *Tall, slender drip glaze vase with handles in multicolored shiny glazes, 12" tall, no mark, $60.00 – 80.00.*

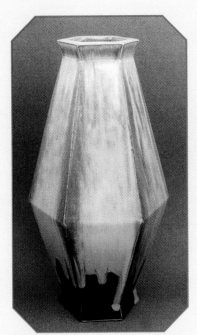

Plate 572. *Tall geometric-shaped drip glaze vase in multicolored shiny glazes, 11¾" tall, no mark, $50.00 – 75.00.*

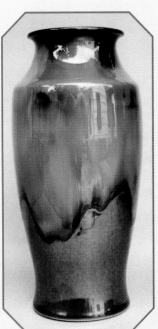

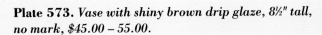

Plate 573. *Vase with shiny brown drip glaze, 8½" tall, no mark, $45.00 – 55.00.*

Plate 574. *Two small vases with shiny brown drip glaze, 3¾" tall, $15.00 – 20.00 each.*

Plate 575. *Large, Gouda-style vase in multicolored shiny glazes, 6½" tall, mark #1, $35.00 – 45.00.*

Plate 576. *Vase with moriage decoration and sprigged-on bird in multicolored shiny glazes, 6¼" tall, red mark #174, $25.00 – 35.00.*

Plate 577. *Large Tokanabe-style vase with bird and floral motif in multicolored semi-matte glaze, 10" tall, blind mark #1, $45.00 – 65.00.*

Plate 578. *Large Tokanabe-style vase in multicolored semi-matte glaze, 10" tall, blind mark #1, $45.00 – 65.00.*

Plate 579. *Hand vase in yellow shiny glaze, 5¾" tall, black mark #2, $15.00 – 25.00.*

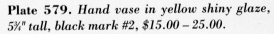

Plate 580. *Majolica-style pierced vase with bird in multicolored semi-matte and shiny glazes, 7½" tall, blind mark #1, $35.00 – 55.00.*

Plate 581. *Boy with bunnies vase in multicolored shiny glazes, 5½" tall, red mark #24, $25.00 – 35.00.*

Plate 582. *Grass shack vase in multicolored shiny glazes, 6¼" tall, blind mark #1, $25.00 – 35.00.*

Plate 583. *Deer vase in multicolored luster and shiny glazes, 6¾" tall, black mark #1, $55.00 – 75.00.*

Plate 584. *Kangaroo vase in multicolored luster and shiny glazes, red mark #56, $55.00 – 75.00.*

Plate 585. *Black swan vase in multicolored luster and shiny glazes, black mark #1, $55.00 – 75.00.*

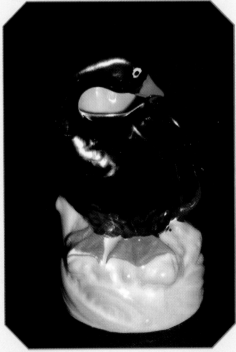

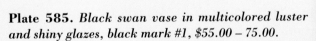

Tree Vases

"Tree" vases have figures on or adjacent to trees. Sometimes the vase comes with a "dimple" on the bottom that can be drilled out for a lamp fitting, and sometimes it comes with a cord hole on the side of the base as well.

Plate 586. *Two tree vases with Native Americans in multicolored luster glazes, pictured in a 1920s – 1930s Butler Brothers wholesale catalog for $.65 wholesale $1.00 – 1.50 retail, both 7¼" tall with black mark, $100.00 – 150.00 each.*

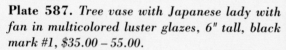

Plate 587. *Tree vase with Japanese lady with fan in multicolored luster glazes, 6" tall, black mark #1, $35.00 – 55.00.*

Plate 588. *Tree vase with Japanese lady in multicolored luster glazes with dimple, 6¼" tall, $35.00 – 55.00.*

Plate 589. *Tree vase with two birds in blue and multicolored luster glazes with dimple and cord hole, 6½" tall, green mark #1, $45.00 – 65.00.*

Plate 590. *Tree vase that has been fitted as a lamp in tan and multicolored luster glazes, 9" to top of socket, black mark #1, $45.00 – 65.00.*

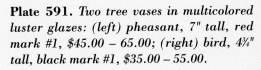

Plate 591. *Two tree vases in multicolored luster glazes: (left) pheasant, 7" tall, red mark #1, $45.00 – 65.00; (right) bird, 4¾" tall, black mark #1, $35.00 – 55.00.*

Plate 592. *Tree vase with bear in multicolored luster and shiny glazes, 7¼" tall, black mark #1, $85.00 – 125.00.*

Plate 593. *Tree vase with dog and owl in multicolored luster and shiny glazes with dimple, 7" tall, black mark #1, $75.00 – 100.00.*

Plate 594. *Noritake tree vase with butterfly in multicolored luster glazes, 5¼" tall, green mark #53, $85.00 – 125.00.*

Plate 595. *Double tree vase with birds in multicolored luster glazes, 3¾" tall, $18.00 – 28.00.*

Plate 596. *Maruyama majolica-style double tree vase in blue and multicolored shiny glazes, 6½" tall, black mark #65, $30.00 – 45.00.*

Plate 597. *Majolica-style double tree vase with birds in cobalt and multicolored shiny glazes, 7½" wide, blind mark #1, $30.00 – 45.00.*

Plate 598. *Majolica-style tree vase with bird in cobalt and multicolored shiny glazes, 8½" tall, blind mark #1, $50.00 – 65.00.*

Wall Pockets

Plate 599. *Banko ware Japanese lady wall pocket in multicolored semi-matte glazes shown in the 1922 Sears Roebuck catalog for $.89, 9" tall, blind mark #1, $65.00 – 100.00.*

Plate 600. *Satsuma-style Japanese lady scenic wall pocket in multicolored semi-matte and shiny glazes with moriage decoration, 5¾" tall, blind mark #121, $95.00 – 125.00.*

Plate 601. *Napco nun wall pockets in multicolored shiny glazes, both 5" tall: (left) "K1717" with silver label; (right) "K1717" with no label; $20.00 – 30.00 each.*

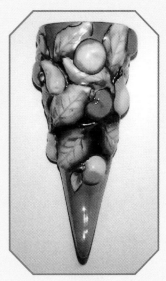

Plate 603. *Fruit wall pocket in multicolored luster glazes, mark removed, $300.00 – 350.00.*

Plate 602. *Bird wall pocket with fruit in multicolored luster glazes, 7¾" tall, $200.00 – 250.00.*

Plate 604. *Blue bird wall pocket in multi-colored luster glazes, 8" tall, red mark #25 with incised Japanese characters, $65.00 – 85.00.*

Plate 605. *White bird with blue crest wall pocket in multicolored luster glazes, 7¾" tall, green mark #25, $65.00 – 85.00.*

Plate 606. *Wall pocket with tan bird in multicolored luster glazes, 6¾" tall, red mark #52, $65.00 – 85.00.*

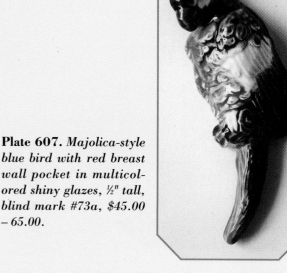

Plate 607. *Majolica-style blue bird with red breast wall pocket in multicolored shiny glazes, ½" tall, blind mark #73a, $45.00 – 65.00.*

Plate 609. *Majolica-style yellow bird on black tree wall pocket in multicolored shiny glazes, 6½" tall, black mark #1, $45.00 – 65.00.*

Plate 608. *Majolica-style yellow bird with red wing wall pocket in multicolored shiny glazes, 7¾" tall, black mark #1, $45.00 – 65.00.*

Plate 611. *Majolica-style bird on brown grapevine wall pocket in multicolored shiny glazes, 7" tall, black mark #1, $45.00 – 65.00.*

Plate 610. *Majolica-style wall pocket with two orange birds, blind mark #73a, $45.00 – 65.00.*

Plate 613. *Majolica-style wall pocket with bird with sweeping blue tail, 8¾" tall, blind mark #73a, $45.00 – 65.00.*

Plate 612. *Majolica-style wall pocket with mama bird and two babies in multicolored shiny glazes, 7¾" tall, blind mark #1, $45.00 – 65.00.*

Plate 614. *Majolica-style bird on gold tree wall pocket in multicolored shiny glazes, 7¼" tall, blind mark #73, $45.00 – 65.00.*

Plate 615. *Majolica-style bird on blue tree wall pocket in multicolored shiny glazes, 9¾" tall, blind mark #172, $45.00 – 65.00.*

Plate 617. *Majolica-style bird with teal breast wall pocket in multicolored shiny glazes, 10" tall, blind mark #1, $45.00 – 65.00.*

Plate 616. *Majolica-style bird with lavender wing tip wall pocket in multicolored shiny glazes, 10" tall, blind marks #172 and #85, $45.00 – 65.00*

Plate 619. *Majolica-style bird on tree wall pocket in pink and multicolored shiny glazes, 8" tall, blind mark #1, $45.00 – 65.00.*

Plate 618. *Majolica-style bird on yellow basket wall pocket in multicolored shiny glazes, 7" tall, black mark #1, $45.00 – 65.00.*

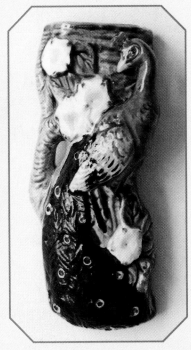

Plate 620. *Majolica-style peacock wall pocket in multicolored shiny glazes, 7¼" tall, blind mark #73, $20.00 – 35.00.*

Plate 621. *Majolica-style owl wall pocket in multicolored shiny glazes, 6¾" tall, blind mark #1, $20.00 – 35.00.*

Plate 622. *Majolica-style wall pocket with cut-out bird in multicolored shiny glazes, 7" tall, black mark #1, $20.00 – 35.00.*

Plate 623. *Majolica-style blue wall pocket with yellow panel in multicolored shiny glazes, 6" tall, blind mark #1, $20.00 – 35.00.*

Plate 624. *Majolica-style bird on basket wall pocket in multicolored shiny glazes, 7½" tall, blind mark #1, $20.00 – 35.00.*

Plate 625. *Majolica-style bird on basket with twig handle wall pocket in multicolored shiny glazes, 7½" tall, no mark, $20.00 – 35.00.*

Plate 626. *Moon vase, which is also a wall pocket, in multicolored shiny glazes, green mark #107, $20.00 – 35.00.*

Plate 627. *Tokanabe-style wall pocket in multicolored semi-matte glazes, 7¾" tall, blind mark #1, $20.00 – 35.00.*

Plate 628. *Tokanabe-style wall pocket in the shape of a vase in multicolored semi-matte glazes, 6" tall, blind mark #1, $20.00 – 35.00.*

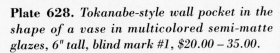

Plate 629. *Blue Majolica-style wall pocket with multicolored mums, 6¼" tall, blue mark #1, $20.00 – 35.00.*

Plate 630. *Sailboat wall pocket in blue and white shiny glazes, 7" tall, black mark #1, $20.00 – 35.00.*

Kitchen Wall Pockets

Plate 631. *Teacup wall pocket in multicolored shiny glazes, 6" diameter, label #59, $20.00 – 35.00.*

Plate 632. *Mixed fruit wall pocket in multicolored shiny glazes, 5" tall, black mark #2, $20.00 – 35.00.*

Plate 633. *Wall pocket with strawberries in multicolored shiny glazes, 7½" tall, silver label faded to unreadability, $20.00 – 35.00.*

Plate 634. *Apple wall pocket in multicolored shiny glazes, 5½" tall, black mark #2, $20.00 – 35.00.*

Plate 635. *Zucchini and tomato wall pocket in multicolored shiny glazes, 4" tall, green mark #28, $20.00 – 35.00.*

Reproductions and Fantasy Items

Plate 636. *Eyeglass holder in multicolored shiny glazes—a fantasy item because it looks like Made in Japan but to our knowledge never was, no mark, but probably had a "Made in China" label, $10.00.*

Plate 637. *Two luster vanity items from China—fantasies because again, they look like they should be original 1920s – 1930s Made in Japan but are from China in 2004. The puff doll on the left has her original "Made in China" tag, but the powder box on the right has no mark or label at all. $15.00 – 20.00 each.*

Plate 638. *Reproduction Satsuma baskets in multicolored shiny glazes, so clever they have even "aged" the bottoms, but the backstamp is Chinese, not Japanese, which means they were made recently and are not antique Satsuma from Japan. $15.00 – 20.00 each.*

Ceramic Novelties, 1960s – 1990s

Prices are wholesale from the period of the catalog.

Selections from a 1965 – 1966 Norcrest Fine Gifts and China Catalog.

Selections from a 1974 Norcrest Fine Gifts and China Catalog.

Selections from a 1989 Norcrest Fine Gifts and China Catalog.

Selections from a 1993 – 1994 Norcrest Fine Gifts and China Catalog.

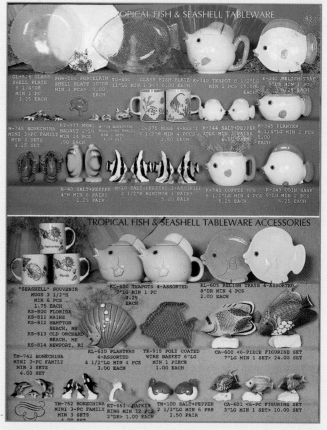

Bibliography

Spain, David, *Noritake Collectibles A TO Z*. Atglen, PA: Schiffer Publishing Ltd., 1997

Van Patten, Joan, *The Collector's Encyclopedia of Nippon Porcelain*. Paducah, KY: Collector Books, 1979.

Van Patten, Joan, *The Collector's Encyclopedia of Noritake*. Paducah, KY: Collector Books, 1984.

White, Carole Bess, *The Collector's Guide to Made in Japan Ceramics*, Volumes 1 – 4. Paducah, KY. Collector Books, 1994 – 2003.

Index

ashtrays 45, 104-116
banks 212
baskets 16, 46, 84-89, 250
bathing beauties 90
berry sugar and cream sets . 62-63, 68
biscuit barrels 47, 91-94, 145
Bonzo 171, 210, 211
bookends 47-48, 95-98
bottle stoppers 161-162
bowls 49, 99-100, 125, 146, 215
boxes 50, 149
bulb bowls 48, 134-138
butter dish 125
cache pots 50-51, 182-189
cake plates/servers 146, 147
calendar 213
calico animals 171, 211, 107
candlestick holders 101-103
candle accessories 103
candy dish 51
candy jars and boxes . . . 51-53, 213
canisters 149-150
cheese keeper 150
child's feeding bowl 215
cigarette/tobacco 16, 53-55,
104-117
clothes brush 212
cocktail pick holders 55, 214
condiment sets 55-56, 118-124
cottage ware 116, 119,
142-143, 196
cream and sugar sets 56, 69-70,
125-126, 147, 150, 151, 154, 200
cup and saucer sets . . 148, 200, 201
decanters 16, 20, 165
divided dish 151

Domino cream and sugar set . . . 150
dresser caddy 213
Drip-o-lator coffee pot 202
dripping jars 147, 154
egg cups 151
egg timers 214-215
eyeglass holder 250
figurines 57-60, 127-133
flasks 166-168
flower bowls 48, 134-138
flower frogs 136, 138-139
gnome 184
Gouda-style 232
humidors 61, 117
incense burners 140-144
instant coffee container 191
jardinière 188
lamps 215-216
lemon servers 216-217
lunch box set 152
liquor items 161-168
majolica-style . . . 88-89, 92-94, 100,
102, 117, 136, 189, 219,
223, 224, 234, 239, 242-246, 248
marmalade or jam pots. 61, 152, 217
match holder 152
mayonnaise sets 61, 169-170
moon vase 247
moriyama kitchenware. . . . 145-148
muffineer sets 62-63, 68,
69, 171-175
napkin holder 153
napkin rings 63, 217-218
nodder 193
nut cups 176-177
pancake/waffle batter set 153

perfume bottles 218-219
pincushions 64, 178-181
pitchers 64, 219
place card holders 65, 220
planters 65, 189
plate 200
powder boxes 66, 190
powder puff 250
range salt and pepper sets. 146, 147,
148, 154-155
salt and pepper sets. 67-68, 125, 146,
147, 148, 151, 154-155, 191-199
salt boxes 147, 148, 153-154
salt dips 176-177
satsuma-style 114, 122, 130
soap dishes 221
spice sets 156-160
spoon holder 68
string holder 221
swagger sticks 222
teapots 69-71, 148, 200-202
thermometer 222
toothbrush holders 203-211
toothpick holders 222
trays 71, 148, 149
tumbler 200
vases
hanging 81, 223-224
standing 71-80, 225-235
tree 236-239
wall plaques 65, 81, 220
wall Pockets . 15, 16, 82-83, 240-249
water set 83
World's Fair 128